RECESSIONS/DEPRESSIONS

FED STYLE

Edward Gale

INFINITY
PUBLISHING

ISBN 0-7414-5928-0

Printed in the United States of America

Published December 2010

INFINITY PUBLISHING
1094 New DeHaven Street, Suite 100
West Conshohocken, PA 19428-2713
Toll-free (877) BUY BOOK
Local Phone (610) 941-9999
Fax (610) 941-9959
Info@buybooksontheweb.com
www.buybooksontheweb.com

For the millions of unemployed who should know the real cause of their shattered lives.

And many, many thanks to Sherry – typist, editor and primary critic for all her hard work.

Table of Contents

Introduction

One question that has endured throughout the economic history of America is: Why have there been so many recessions or depressions? Can't America learn from its previous economic mistakes and avoid such disastrous events? Apparently not as the financial collapse of 2008 so vividly shows.

There is the popular belief that recessions or depressions are caused by irresponsible Wall Street bankers. This belief has been recently reinforced by the 2008 financial collapse.

Economists who study quantitative items such as production figures, prices and wages, inflation rates and so forth to ascertain the workings of the business cycle, offer a more economically technical cause for these events such as disequilibrium between the money supply and workers' wages.

And some economists believe that recessions are a normal part of all business cycles occurring whenever demand lessens and business inventories rise. In essence, lower selling means decreasing business means recession.

In this study, however, after examining American recessions and depressions significantly affecting economic activity, it was surprising to find that the Federal government or Federal Reserve Board were directly involved in providing the economic expansive conditions that seem to always precede the inevitable contractions. And, more times than not, it was for political gain that the expansive conditions were produced (although sometimes expansion was necessary during wars). The usual means for expansion were tax cuts, subsidies and welfare programs all having the added effect of ingratiating the politicians with the voters.

Political gain, as every politician worth their salt knows, involves the pocketbook of unsophisticated voters. While America would like to think it votes for such abstractions as leadership, character, patriotism, etc., it has always voted its pocketbook. Any political party or President in charge at the time a recession or depression erupts is always voted out of office at the very next election as Martin Van Buren (1837-1841) and Herbert Hoover (1929-1933) found out.

This has always been the way in democracies. The ancient Greek philosopher Plato (427?-347? BC) supposedly observed that democracies go bankrupt because their citizens continuously vote for the politician who promises the most government handouts. No goodies, no vote is what it amounts to.

In relation to recessions or depressions, even with historical precedent, it is despicable that American politicians have produced expansive economic conditions apparently to keep their jobs and keep their party in power regardless of the economic misery inflicted on the working class when the expansive conditions get out of hand and the economy implodes.

While economists generally study recessions or depressions individually, this study will emphasize the longer expansive causes of the inevitable contraction that follows. It will also show that periods of expansion do not always end in one dramatic recession or depression such as the Great Depression of 1930-1941. Often, periods of expansion stumble to an end with several minor-to-severe recessions separated by smaller expansive times.

Also of note with recessions and depressions is the psychology underpinning the events. During expansion, as the money supply increases, consumer spending increases, production picks up, business expands and more workers are hired. Times are good; the public feels upbeat about the future. The more ambitious take the expansive opportunity to make money – often a lot of money and often recklessly. Their optimism soon changes to exuberance as the expansive boom continues. Therein lies the problem: human nature. Exuberance leads some, however, to the disconcerting belief that the good times have lasted too long. A psychological doubt begins to grow even with the optimists but especially with the pessimists. At that point, any little spark can start the implosion and the rush to the exits.

Speculators, big investors, followed by the little investors all rush to get their paper profits out of the stock market. With everyone selling, the market naturally collapses. Psychological doubt becomes the motivator. Consumers cut back their purchases, production falls, business and banks hunker down, unemployment rises and the preceding good times become bad times – a recession. Depending on the height of the psychological exuberance, the fall back to reality can develop into a long and deep depression. The very word describes the psychological mood of the country.

The economic misery of the hard times brings into question the morality of the Federal government in attempting to stimulate the economy for the "good" of the public not to mention the morality of the politicians using stimulus packages to buy votes as some critics charge.

This treatise will show just how involved the Federal government and the Federal Reserve Board have been in the misery of recessions or depressions. The old saw "there is no free lunch" is never truer than when dealing with politicians' promises. A massive tax cut promised by a Presidential candidate might sound good to the average unsophisticated voter but what will be its miserable effect three, four, five years in the future when the stimulated economy can no longer be controlled? In the following pages, we shall see what has happened all too often in the past.

Chapter One

The Early Years 1775-1865

Revolutionary War (1775-1783) During the war, the states spent upwards of 40 million dollars – a huge sum at that time. This spending for war supplies and weapons supported a barely-adequate economy for the young country. With the end of the war, most of the spending stopped; money became scarce, and wide scale bartering in rural areas was the rule. Trade, the lifeblood of the colonies, especially with England, was slow to recover. With no revenue, the states began issuing paper money, resulting in inflation. For its first fledgling years, America was in a deep depression. The same result occurred after every American war in the decades and centuries ahead when war funding was curtailed.

What didn't decrease during this first depression were taxes, especially on farms whose owners, unable to pay, often lost their farms and were thrown in jail as debtors. Daniel Shays, a Massachusetts farmer and former army captain, fought back with a ragtag band of farmers. In the late summer of 1786, they raided court debtors' trials and disrupted the sale of confiscated farms. If anything good came out of this early depression, it was the fear that Shay's rebellion put into the state leaders prompting them to scrap the weak Confederacy the states were operating under and write a new constitution for a strong central government. The Constitution Convention delegates met in Philadelphia in September 1787. They wrote the Constitution and had it ratified by all the states in less than three years. It was, John Adams believed, "the greatest single effort of national deliberation that the world has ever seen."

John Adams (1797-1801) For the first twenty-five years of its existence, the United States was beset by fears of war with England as well as France. The economy directly paralleled these fears, rising when war clouds dissipated, falling into a recession or depression when war clouds gathered. In 1793, shortly after George Washington began his second term as president, the newly formed French Republic declared war on England. This raised havoc with American shipping as sailors were impressed and ships seized by the two warring nations. Washington tried an embargo on trade with the two countries for a few months to avoid war but this caused a minor recession in 1793.

Washington next tried negotiating a neutrality pact with England that wasn't successful in stopping the seizure of ships but he signed it (reluctantly) to stay out of war. This abrogated an earlier solidarity pact made with the pre-Republic France. Thomas Jefferson and his Francophile followers were angered and reviled Washington as a tyrant and dictator. France was also angered enough to increase the seizing of American ships. Nevertheless, the signing of the treaty with England lifted war fears in the country and the economy surged, reaching a peak of activity shortly before the 1796 election.

John Adams won the Presidency over Thomas Jefferson in a close contest (71 electoral votes to 68) perhaps because of the economic surge preceding the election. No sooner had he entered office, however, than the fear of war returned this time with France as more and more US ships were seized. From 1797 to 1799, the country was in a recession/depression. Adams's attempt to negotiate with the French broke down when the French demanded a ten million dollar loan and $250,000 for the negotiators. America turned against their former Revolutionary War ally declaring "millions for defense, not one cent for tribute." Jefferson and his followers severely criticized Adams and his Federalist party for the war crisis.

At the height of the war fears, the Federalist Congress passed the Alien and Sedition Act allowing for the imprisonment or expulsion of foreign aliens. In addition, no one was allowed to criticize the country, the government or the Presidency. Jefferson was incensed with this law. He declared the act unconstitutional, writing that because the states had existed before the Federal government and had indeed formed the government and ratified the Constitution, they could nullify any law they found unconstitutional. This thinking became the basis for southern states nullifying tariff laws in 1832 and seceding from the Union in 1861.

Thomas Jefferson (1801-1809) With war fears and a parallel recession/depression lingering throughout most of John Adam's single four-year term, it is no surprise the he lost the 1800 election to Jefferson. America has always voted their pocketbooks ousting

Presidents and parties associated with recession and depressions. America has also always voted for Presidential candidates promising to keep the country out of wars, as in the case of Woodrow Wilson in 1916 and Franklin D. Roosevelt in 1940. So poor John Adams never really stood a chance in the 1800 election. Both the economy and war fears were against him.

Adams did manage to re-establish trade with France toward the end of his term with a treaty signed in September 1800. But it was too late for him to reap any political advantage. Jefferson, a known Francophile, on the other hand, saw a large spike in economic activity his first year in office (1801).

The rest of his first term, however, the economy struggled through a recession/depression (1802-1804) caused by the four-year struggle with the Barbary Coast pirates and the increasing tensions between England and Napoleonic France, which interrupted America trade with Europe.

Jefferson's second term (1805-1809), however, buoyed up by the fact that he kept the US out of the European battles, saw the highest level of economic activity in the 1800s. The good times came to an abrupt end in 1807 as well as Jefferson's popularity when he signed the Embargo Act to stop England and France who were fighting again from seizing American ships and impressing US seamen. The act closed American ports to foreign ships and prohibited American shipping to Europe. However, instead of forcing England and France to stop their high seas predatory practices, it was America that suffered economically almost immediately – the country went into a sharp depression. Eastern commerce dried up, the farm products of the South and West had no buyers. Exports, which were at $108 million in 1807, sank to only $22 million in 1808.

Federalist New England was furious, the South and West equally so. Jefferson was vilified in the press, especially Federalist newspapers. Angry at the attacks, he decided a third term wasn't worth it and chose to honor George Washington's lead of only serving two terms. Before leaving office, Jefferson repealed the embargo in 1809 providing James Madison (1809-1817) with a one-year upswing in economic activity (1811) but still leaving him with the problem of how to deal with the English and French seizure of US shipping. Negotiations succeeded with the French and trade resumed but England continued to seize ships and seamen, so Madison declared war on England (June 18,1812).

This disrupted all foreign trade and quickly a recession/depression followed (1812-1815).

So, because of foreign wars in Europe, first Thomas Jefferson and then James Madison inadvertently triggered severe recessions or depressions in America. And, like all such dismal economic events in America to follow, it wasn't the well-to-do who suffered but rather it was farmers, workers, shopkeepers (the little people) who suffered the worst by losing their jobs, their savings and their dreams of getting ahead in the world.

Unfortunately, it didn't get any better economically for the little people from the years 1819 to 1830 during the terms of James Monroe (1817-1825) and John Quincy Adams (1825-1829). Except for a few years (1825-1826) at the start of Adam's term when activity picked up, the rest of the period was in the red.

Sectionalism riled the nation then and brought economic uncertainty. The mid-Atlantic manufacturing states wanted high protective tariffs, northeastern merchants opposed it. Western states wanted government-paid roads, eastern interests opposed it. The South wanted to expand slavery into the Louisiana Purchase Territory, the North opposed it. Until the country's direction was clearer, the economy struggled.

Andrew Jackson (1829-1837) The next President to trigger a depression was Andrew Jackson. Unfortunately for the country, it was a severe, long-lasting one regarded as being second in misery only to the Great Depression of the 1930s.

Jackson was an impulsive, arrogant, egotistical fellow, ambitious and competitive to the core. He sought no counsel, always believing he was right. In modern parlance, he would be considered a macho male, quick to take offense, quick to fight (he was a renown duelist during his younger years in Tennessee), quick to hold a grudge and quick to hate his political enemies (of which there were many). In old age, when asked if he had any regrets, he is reported to have said: "only two, that he had not shot Clay nor hung Calhoun."

He also hated the English. His two elder brothers died in the Revolutionary War and he, himself, had been brutally slashed with a sword by a British officer.

As a western shopkeeper and landowner, the eastern establishment rich bluebloods who controlled the banks and finances of the country were also high on his hatred list. In fact, it was this animosity toward the eastern establishment that would eventually lead to his triggering of the 1837 bank panic and following depression that had lingering effects until 1847.

When Jackson first ran for President in 1824, even though he received the most votes of the four candidates (including John Quincy Adams and Henry Clay) he didn't receive a majority necessary for election. In the House of Representatives' vote to determine the winner, Henry Clay released his votes to Adams which insured Adam's election. When Adams named Clay his Secretary of State, Jackson and his followers were outraged declaring that a deal had been made stealing the election from Jackson. Both Adams, an eastern blueblood, and Clay, who supported the bluebloods, were henceforth Jackson's enemies.

The 1828 election between Adams and Jackson became an "aristocrats versus the people" campaign with smears and slurs flying from each side. It didn't help Adams that the country was in a recession/depression. Like his father John Adams, John Quincy became another President escorted to the door by voters cognizant of their pocketbooks.

It is difficult to say just when, in Jackson's first term, his hatred of the eastern bluebloods directed his attention towards not renewing the charter of the Bank of the United States; the bank was the symbol of the eastern control of the country's financial system. Apparently Jackson had made his distain for the bank known some time before the 1832 election because Henry Clay, his Presidential opponent in the election, decided to force the bank issue to recharter it (the charter was to run out in 1836) as a means of gaining an advantage in the campaign. Thinking that Jackson would veto any recharter, Clay and his followers in Congress voted for an early renewal bill for the bank in 1832. Jackson did veto the bill but he couched his veto in such patriotic terms and common-man hyperbole (the bank would "make the rich richer") that Clay's scheme backfired. The unsophisticated voters were all for eliminating the bank and getting a share of the economic pie, so they voted overwhelmingly for Jackson.

Jackson believed his re-election a mandate to eliminate the bank so he proceeded in 1833 to remove all the Federal funds from the bank, asking his Secretary of the Treasury to do so and deposit the funds in the state banks around the country. When the secretary refused, Jackson dismissed him, appointing another secretary who also refused. A third secretary finally removed the funds amid cries of "tyrant," "dictator," "King Andrew" from his opponents now called Whigs, (an allusion to the colonial Whigs who opposed the English king and the Tories during the Revolutionary War). For his high-handed and what many considered unconstitutional actions, the Senate censured Jackson in 1834. Jackson's actions also created fear in the eastern banking system plunging the country into an economic downspin (1833-35).

The dispersal of Federal funds throughout the country, however, was a windfall for the banking industry. Whereas in 1829 there had been 329 banks, by 1837 there were 788 banks. Jackson had long believed that the small western banks that lent to settlers, farmers, workers and shopkeepers (all Jackson followers) were often denied loans from the larger eastern banks and the Bank of the United States as being too speculative. With the dispersal of the Federal funds, the small state banks could lend and lend they did especially to land speculators buying up potential farmland from the government which was selling land to encourage western settlement. It was a "land-office business" with parcels of land often changing speculators' hands a dozen times before settlers or farmers would buy them at an inflated price.

As the money came into the government land office, it was deposited in state banks that lent it out as quickly as it came in, often to more speculators buying more government land. It was a vicious circle, often with the speculators keeping the best land for themselves. All the lending and buying produced an economic boom. Money was no longer dear; it became an easy money time. Trade picked up and inflation followed stimulating business, hiring of workers and consumer spending even for luxury items such as silk from England.

As the inflation rose, the American dollar dropped in value prodding foreign exporters to demand payment in hard money. Gold flowed out of the country to the point where it became dangerously low.

Not being an economist and unheedful of advice, Jackson probably had no idea that his headstrong decision to strip the Bank of the United States of its Federal funds would create such an expansive atmosphere. He also probably didn't realize that in such an atmosphere, a psychological "irrational exuberance" (Alan Greenspan's term 160 years later) takes control leading to reckless lending and speculative investing. Everyone wanted to get rich as soon as possible, as long as the good times rolled. Banks overextended themselves, businesses expanded and hired to meet the inflated demand for goods, and consumers with more money in their pockets were indiscriminate in their purchases.

In an expansive atmosphere, in such a land office "bubble," it takes only the smallest pin to burst the bubble and start a crashing contraction. And Andrew Jackson fittingly supplied the pin in his headstrong fashion. First, angered by the fact that the speculators were ending up with the most valuable land and charging settlers and farmers inflated prices for poorer land, he put out a *Specie Circular* in July 1836 declaring that after August 15, 1836, the government would not accept paper money for land – payment was to be in gold or silver only.

A few months later, Jackson dropped the second shoe with the Distribution Act declaring that beginning January 1, 1837, the Federal funds deposited in the state banks had to be repaid in gold or silver. The banks were suddenly in a pickle. The Federal funds had all been lent out beyond their own regular reserves. They counted on the continuous deposit of funds from the booming land sales to keep a running reserve. But the *Specie Circular* had cooled those sales and the redepositing of Federal funds had ended.

Somehow the banks met the first January payment but could not meet the second in April. Banks began to fail, business contracted, consumer buying decreased. The Panic of 1837 deepened into a depression the next two years that was soon exported abroad. In England, for example, those businesses that could not collect their American debt went bankrupt. England's business activity dropped, banks stopped lending, and cotton mills closed which, in turn, brought down the price of American cotton. This reduced the buying power of the South decreasing its purchase of the West's farm products. Completing the circle, the West stopped buying eastern manufactured products shutting down factories and laying off workers.

So Jackson's headstrong actions to cripple the US Bank and at the same time help western settlers and farmers buy needed land produced a strong expansion followed by a sharp contraction. This helped neither the little man nor the country nor foreign countries. The misery was spread around indiscriminately. Newspaper drawings depicted widows and children begging for food, shops for sale, runs on banks, factories closed, unemployment lines and sheriffs auctioning off foreclosed farms.

Poor Martin Van Buren, the handpicked successor of Andrew Jackson. He had been handily elected in the land-office boom times of 1835-36 but he had barely taken office in March 1837 when the results of all of Jackson's bank finagling came crashing down on him in May. By summer, the country was in a depression. Somehow, through printing more money, he managed a brief recovery of economic activity in 1838 but when the Bank of the United States (the very same bank that Jackson set out to cripple) failed in 1839, the country fell into a deep depression that lasted until 1845 and dampened the economy until 1847. It was a stiff price for the country to pay because of one man's obsession to ruin a bank.

True to form, the country voted out Martin Van Buren as soon as it could. In 1840, the Whigs' (all Jackson haters) candidate William Harrison ("ol Tippecanoe and Tyler too" – John Tyler as Veep) won the President's office. Even though the Harrison line seemed to have a healthy constitution (he had 10 children, 48 grand children and 106 great-grand children), he caught a cold while delivering one of the longest inaugural speeches ever. The cold developed into pneumonia and he died a month later. At least he didn't have to face the financial mess his successor John Tyler did. (Tyler had 15 children by two wives – when did these Whigs find time for politics?) The severe depression lasted throughout his four-year term hitting rock bottom in 1843. Again, the voters voted their pocketbooks giving Tyler his walking papers. The winner of the election in 1844 was James K. Polk, a Democrat. Jackson's party was again in control thanks to the ongoing depression ironically triggered by Jackson ten years earlier. Also ironically, it toppled the Whigs.

The country finally got out of the depression when it declared war on Mexico (1846-48) because it had refused to sell the land between Texas and California. The convenient reason was that Mexican troops had invaded US territory. Wars, with their stimulating effect on the economy, are a sure-fire way to change recessions and depressions to economically positive recovery periods. The one exception in the country's history was the Civil War that devastated the South's economy.

Minor recessions were the rule from 1858 to 1865 with two minor recovery periods (1859-60 and 1864). The Dred Scott Supreme Court decision (1857) declaring that slaves as property were protected by the Constitution outraged the abolitionist North. Commerce between North and South decreased throwing the country into a recession (1858). After secession in 1861, commerce fell again. Without the South's cotton and tobacco revenue being spent in the North and West, money became dear and the government had to print "greenbacks" to finance the war.

Plotting on a graph the economic activity for America during its early years from 1775 to 1865, it becomes apparent that America suffered from more years in recession or depressions than in periods of economic growth. Many of those negative economic years were caused by the aftermath of wars, or European wars impacting our trade, or by direct actions of leaders such as President Jefferson with his disastrous Embargo Act and Andrew Jackson with his land-office boom policies. So, while the country grew geographically and population rose, its economic growth wasn't that robust with several periods of recessions or depressions.

Chapter Two

Industrial Expansion 1865-1914

The "Long Depression" (1873-1879) The first widespread expansion in the Industrial Revolution started after the Civil War. In order to facilitate the settlement of the West and to hook up the western states to the rest of the country, Congress passed the Pacific Railroad Bill (1862, amended 1864) to provide loans, subsidies and right-of-way grants to private railroad companies. Whenever the Federal government is giving away money or land, everyone wants a piece of the "golden eagle." Soon new railroad companies were sprouting up like spring flowers; banks and speculators rushed into investing in railroad companies. After all, it was a sure thing – the government was practically guaranteeing no risk with its loans and outright subsidies to build the railroad tracks. The "exuberance" spread to other industries. The over-building of factories, storage facilities, bridges, loading docks soon followed.

The expansive economic activity helped elect Ulysses S. Grant as President (1869-1877). During his time in office, the country was divided. Farmers, small businesses and debtors wanted to return to the bimetallic (gold and silver) money in circulation before the Civil War believing that would raise farm prices and make paying their debts easier. The eastern financial interests, however, wanted only a gold standard that would stabilize prices and allow their loans to be repaid at full value. Grant and Congress finally sided with the financiers, passing the Coinage Act of 1873 that had the immediate effect of making money scarce because it stopped the purchase of silver, the minting of silver dollars and the redemption in silver of any paper money.

The farmers and debtors were outraged by this concession to the eastern "fat cats." Economic activity, which had been expansive (even excessively so), dropped. Investors and speculators became wary of long-term investment in such agitated times. Banks that had over-extended themselves in loans propping up the railroad "balloon," began calling in risky loans and curtailing lending.

In these financially uncertain times after the Coinage Act, the Jay Cooke and Company bank, heavily involved in the building of a transcontinental railroad, the Northern Pacific Railway, crashed in September 1873. They couldn't sell long-term Northern Pacific bonds to stabilize their reserves and continue building. Word got out that they were in trouble and a run on the bank ensued. Soon other over-extended banks had to deal with runs and many failed.

Credit dried up and economic activity spiraled down into a depression. Some ninety railroads went bankrupt and over 10,000 businesses closed their doors; by 1876, unemployment was at 14%. Real estate and land decreased in value eventually across the entire county. With scarce money and no credit, there was nowhere for the economy to go but down into six years of what was called the "Long Depression." Labor strife in 1877 helped to prolong the depression as striking railroad workers and Federal troops clashed resulting in over 100 dead.

With the country's interest focused on the depression, interest in the government's reconstruction efforts in the South waned. It was reported that in the tied election of 1876 between the Republican Hayes and the Democrat Tilden, a Republican-weighed commission to pick the winner chose Hayes. The Democrats were outraged. They threatened "Tilden or blood!" To placate the Democrats, especially the southern Democrats, the Republicans agreed to pull all Federal troops out of the South in return for a Hayes victory.

The southerners soon reasserted themselves, once more assigning blacks to second-class status after Federal troops were pulled out in 1876. The blacks would have to wait almost a hundred years before their rights were asserted again.

In many aspects, the 1873-79 depression paralleled the depression of 1837-45. Both started out as economically expansive periods generated by the Federal government's largesse: the Federal loans, subsidies and land grants to build railroads for the former and Andrew Jackson's distribution of Federal funds to state banks to enable settlers to buy land for the latter.

Both increases in the money supply led to irrational exuberance in the economy with overextension in bank lending. Speculators increased risky investments, a building boom ensued, inflated land and real estate values spread, and eventually damaging inflation resulted.

And the bubbles produced in railroad building (late 1860s) and land sales (mid 1830s) were both exploded by the deflationary effects of returning to hard currency. The Coinage Act of 1873 returned the country to the gold standard while the *Specie Circular* demanded gold or silver for land sales and the Distribution Act 1836) required banks to repay Federal funds in gold or silver.

Both deflationary events made money scarce, forcing overly extended banks into failure and thereby freezing credit between banks and businesses. The end result was business bankruptcies, worker layoffs and long, economically miserable depressions.

The 1873-79 depression finally ended only after the Federal Congress passed the Bland-Allison Act in 1878 returning the US to a bimetallic standard. The 1837-45 events ended with Congress declaring war on Mexico. As can be seen, the Fed's fingerprints are all over these two depressions from start to finish. One would think that after two Fed-caused depressions, the Congress or the President would have learned that anytime the Federal government provides a monetary stimulus to the economy, no matter the reason, a recession or depression is the inevitable result.

One also has to wonder here about the political timing of the Bland-Allison Act of 1878 returning the country to silver coins and silver certificates (paper money redeemable in silver). The Republicans had been in charge during the Long Depression and knew that if the economy didn't improve, they would lose the 1880 Presidential election. Was it really for the good of the country and the downtrodden that they passed a bill expanding the money supply? Or were they thinking privately that the grateful public would vote for them in 1880? While some may think this is too cynical a way of thinking, others think that one can never be too cynical when it comes to the motives of politicians.

1883-1885 Depression As soon as the 1878 Bland-Allison Act started pouring silver into the money supply, it not only ended the Long Depression years but it also started a new expansive period (1879-82). And just as in the expansion years preceding the Long Depression, banks, investors and speculators again started investing recklessly in railroads and construction. One would think that after going through a six-year depression only four years earlier that "caution" would be the watchword in investing again, especially in the railroads. Were they stupid, innately reckless or just greedy?

In any case, almost the same series of events happened again. The easy money atmosphere, the good times exuberance led to overexpansion in credit, business growth and employee hiring far beyond what the system could handle if anything unforeseen happened. Over extended, the economy was still receiving 2-4 million silver dollars every month as the 1878 Bland-Allison Act stipulated. By 1884, 27 million silver dollars had been introduced.

The good times abruptly changed in 1883 when there was talk in government circles of going off the silver standard. That, combined with the fact that the banks had been paying back their Treasury loans with abundant silver rather than scarce gold, had given other countries the impression that the US banks were hoarding their gold because they feared the Feds might be considering abandoning the gold standard. Foreigners began selling their US securities demanding gold in payment thereby draining US stocks. Because by law there had to be a strict ratio of gold to every gold-backed dollar, a decline in the gold stocks meant a decline in the gold-backed money supply. The silver removal talk and the gold drain meant scarce money ahead and banks tried to shore up their reserves by calling in loans. Such a loss of psychological exuberance dampened business expansion and reined in railroad building.

On May 8, 1884, with the economy already collapsing, the New York City brokerage firm Grant and Ward (former President Grant's firm) failed after one of their checks for $750,000 was refused payment at a major bank leading depositors to think that the bank didn't have enough funds to cover it – and the run was on. Worried depositors all over the city rushed to withdraw their money. It didn't help matters when a rumor circulated that one bank president had absconded with 3 million dollars. Forty-two banks failed in May alone. Credit dried up, business contracted (nearly 10,000 businesses failed), farm prices fell by 50%, farmers lost their land and unemployment soared. In the manufacturing northeast, unemployment hit 13% as opposed to a normal 2.5%. Railroad construction declined from 11,500 miles in 1882 to 2,800 miles in 1885. Even road construction declined from 750,000 miles in 1882 to 400,000 miles in 1885 as jobs disappeared.

President Chester A. Arthur, who had stepped into the Presidency in 1881 after the elected Republican President James A. Garfield had been assassinated by a disgruntled office seeker, told Congress in his State of the Union message of 1884 that trade had to be increased to get the country out of the depression. The Republican protective high tariffs, however, wouldn't let that happen because retaliatory foreign tariffs kept trade at a minimum.

This time the Republicans couldn't escape responsibility for the financial mess. After all, during the 1884 Presidential election, the country was deep in the depression. Once again Americans voted their pocketbooks and threw the Republican "scoundrels" out. The new President Grover Cleveland, a Democrat, was just the man the country needed. He believed firmly in the gold standard and thought "cheap" silver money led to financial disaster. He attacked high tariffs and vetoed "give-away" pension plans for Civil War veterans as being too extravagant. His fiscally responsible administration restored the country's confidence; by 1885, economic activity increased and the depression faded away.

The years 1885-1888 were good economic years without any over expansion but by the Presidential election of 1888, the voters had forgotten the financial hardships under the last Republican administration. In addition, the angry veteran groups whose pensions Cleveland had vetoed, campaigned vigorously against him. The high tariff-supporters favored the Republican candidate Benjamin Harrison (one of "Tippecanoe and Tyler too" President William Harrison's 48 grandchildren). In addition, the farmers and silverists disliked Cleveland for his strong anti-silver stand.

To get elected, Harrison and the Republicans promised the vets their pensions, the protectionists their high tariffs, and the farmers and silverites their coins. Naturally, the unsophisticated American voter elected Harrison over Cleveland. There is a corollary to the axiom that in a democracy, voters always vote out the party believed to be associated with a recession or depression. As Plato warned, voters also always vote for the candidate or party promising the most handouts from the Federal Treasury. So, in 1888, a perfectly sound, fiscally responsible Democratic President was voted out of office for a fiscally irresponsible Republican President.

1893-1897 Depression As soon as Harrison and the Republicans entered office in 1889, they started making good on their expansive promises. The veterans' pensions were doubled, the McKinley Tariff Act of 1890 gladdened the protectionists and the Silver Purchase Act placated farmers and the silver interests. All this Federal largesse helped the economy to take off. Millions of dollars were poured into the economy. Lending began in earnest again to the railroads and construction; businesses expanded and hired more workers. It was the same expansive, exuberant scenario all over again. Government increased expenditures on internal improvements like roads, bridges, etc. added to the construction frenzy. The Republican Congress came to be pejoratively called the "Billion Dollar Congress."

Ironically, in the middle of these "good times," the government found it was having trouble paying its bills. The Federal surplus from Cleveland's term had disappeared with all the handouts and the fact that revenue, after the high McKinley Tariff Act passed, fell sharply as retaliatory foreign tariffs kicked in. In the 1890 mid-term election, the Republicans lost the House of Representatives to the Democrats. Still, after a short recession immediately following the election, the good times roared on.

Signs of the inevitable decline of the Republican bubble didn't start showing up until shortly before the 1892 Presidential election. For some time, the farmers reacting to the rising prices of the boom planted more and more acres. Eventually they flooded their markets with a surplus which drove down farm prices. Also, foreign investors, seeing all the silver pouring into the American economy after the Sherman Silver Purchase Act of 1890, feared a loss of value in their US securities and began selling, demanding gold in payment. And just as in previous depressions, this payment of gold to foreigners drained the gold supply decreasing gold-backed dollars because of the legal ratio requirements – the higher the gold supply, the more dollars can be printed, the lower, the less dollars.

Once the psychological doubts enter the minds of the financially sophisticated, any little financial disturbance can blow up the whole system. Again, it was the overbuilt, over leveraged railroads. The Philadelphia and Reading Railroad went bankrupt on February 2, 1893. Soon, the Northern Pacific Railway, the Union Pacific Railroad and the Atchison, Topeka and Santa Fe line followed suit. And as usual, as we have seen in every Federal induced expansion leading to a depression, the run on the banks started, credit collapsed, businesses failed and workers were laid off. At the depth of the depression, 17-19% of the work force was unemployed, 15,000 companies gave up the ghost and some 500 banks failed mostly out west. Farm foreclosures ballooned.

The irony here is that during Harrison's expansive term (1889-93) and the Billion Dollar Congress, labor strife, worker strikes and the farmers' continuous agitation for more silver turned public sentiment against the Republicans as economic activity sagged in the second half of 1892. This, combined with the growing wealth of the industrial and financial "plutocrats" with their "pool" and "trusts" schemes to increase profits while denying workers any wage raises, elected Grover Cleveland, the Democrat, to a second term in 1892. Cleveland was just about to enter office when the Republican largesse expansion period imploded with the railroad bankruptcies in February 1893. With his anti-silver beliefs that too much silver caused economic chaos, he quickly had the new Congress repeal the Sherman Silver Purchase Act (enacted only three years earlier). This impulsive act not only destroyed the western silver mines, laying off thousands of miners, but it didn't help alleviate the depression. Reducing the silver money in an already crashing economy in which credit is drying up and money is becoming scarcer by the day requires, as we now know today, pumping money into the economy. If anything, removing silver at the depth of the depression only prolonged it.

Eventually Cleveland's style of financial frugality was more of a hindrance than a help in promoting recovery. Whereas in 1885, his firm fiscal policies had helped the country get out of the 1883-85 depression, the same policies at the start of the deep 1893 depression weren't as helpful. To make matters worse, Cleveland had to borrow $65 million in gold from the plutocrat banker J. P. Morgan just to shore up the Treasury's supply of gold. Doing business with the "enemy" so to speak didn't endear him to the public nor did his blunt manner in dealing with labor unrest – police and the military were called out to violently disperse the agitators.

But the real irony was the fact that the public and press blamed him for starting the depression. Neither Grover Cleveland nor the Democrats had any hand in starting the 1893-97 depression. It was all Benjamin Harrison and the Billion Dollar Republican Congress in their largesse in veteran's pensions and silver purchases that created the expansive mentality in the economy during Harrison's term (1889-93). One would think that the American voter could remember that just four years previously which political party had provoked a boom for their own political advantage.

But they didn't. McKinley, the Republicans and the "gold bugs" won the 1896 election by some 600,000 votes not withstanding the Democratic candidate William Jennings Bryant's famous "Cross of Gold" speech "you shall not crucify mankind upon a cross of gold."

In the previous 1894-midterm election, the country in the deep depression voted overwhelmingly against the Democrats. It was clear that the public blamed the Democrats for the depression, so McKinley, in 1896, ran on a "full dinner pail" platform, emphasizing the "prosperity" in the last Republican period – Harrison's Billion Dollar Congress.

The major policy issue of 1896 though was the single gold standard favored by the Republicans and their campaign contributors, the financial and industrial plutocrats versus a bimetallic (silver and gold) standard favored by the Democrats and their farmer, miner and worker supporters. In other words, the plutocrats versus the people. To the former, the gold standard meant a stable currency, steady growth and above all, full dollar value when debtors repaid their debts – inflated silver dollars meant smaller true profits. To the Democrats and populace, a gold standard meant scarce money, low prices for farmers and low wages – a lid on prosperity and growth.

In actuality, a gold standard did bring stability but if there wasn't enough gold in the Treasury's vaults, it made money scarce and dampened prosperity because legally there had to be a definite gold reserve backing each gold dollar. Much of the gold in the country at that time sat in the vaults of the plutocrats (as seen with J. P. Morgan's loan of $65 million in gold to the government) so that it wasn't available to back expanding the Federal money supply.

And it is also true that silver brought instability and inflation to the system but it wasn't because of its intrinsic value. Rather, the instability resulted from the politicians first flooding the economy with silver and then abruptly taking it away often for their own political advantage. The often-noted "roller coaster" economy of the latter half of the 19th Century correlates almost perfectly with the practice of inserting and then removing silver from the economy.

It would have been far better economically if, after the Civil War, Congress would have allowed a bimetallic standard that everyone – plutocrat and the people – could have gotten used to, diminishing uncertainty and promoting stability.

The way the economy played out, however, was like a favorite uncle taking his nieces and nephews to a candy store every four or five years and telling them to eat as much as they wanted. Of course, they gorged and got sick but when the uncle shows up a few years later, the kids don't remember the sickness only the wonderful taste of the candy. The kids would actually look forward to the next exuberance of plenty.

So William Jennings Bryant was right – the people were being crucified on the plutocratic cross of gold (usually helped by the Republicans). What he didn't seem to realize or didn't want to admit was that the people voluntarily flocked to the cross for a piece of the action. They had bought into the plutocrats' propaganda that if you worked hard, you would succeed, enter the middle class and be a property owner. Of course the propaganda didn't mention that you had to work for indecent wages and much of the time in unsafe conditions. No one seemed to mention that the middle class goal could also be reached in a stable economy with decent wages for the people and only reasonable profits for the plutocrats. Of course, then they wouldn't be plutocrats.

William McKinley was lucky in the 1896 election; he ran against a political party tarred with the depression of the four previous years. He got even luckier shortly after taking office. Recent gold discoveries in Alaska and Australia plus the invention of the cyanide extraction process allowing more gold to come from South Africa, flooded the world with new gold. This enabled the US and other countries on the gold standard to increase their money in circulation giving a boost to their economies. For the US, this meant a natural way out of the depression with a steady increase in economic activity tempered by a few minor recessions until 1903.

Winning the Spanish-American War in 1898 also aided McKinley's popularity as did his running with Theodore Roosevelt (the hero of San Juan Hill during the war) on the Republican ticket in 1900. His luck, however, ran out in September 1902 when he was assassinated by an anarchist. Theodore "Teddy" Roosevelt became the 26th President of the United States at the very young age of 42.

1907-1909 Depression The economic recovery after the 1893-97 depression, due mainly to the currency inflationary influence of all the new gold supplies worldwide in the late 1890s, proceeded at a quickening pace during McKinley's first term (1897-1901) and Roosevelt's first term (1902-1905). As usual, in a fast-paced recovery, exuberance overtook rationality – banks over lent, businesses over expanded and unemployment fell. Roosevelt, at this time, began the government's first anti-trust case (1902); 44 were to follow during his time in office. That, and his firm hand in bringing about a negotiated settlement (mostly in favor of the coal miners) between the miners and the coal companies endeared him to the public. So even though the country experienced another recession in 1903-05, Roosevelt won his second term in 1904 by a record 2.5 million votes (or a 56% to 35% ratio) over Alton Parker. Not until Warren Harding, another Republican, defeated James Cox in 1920 by a 61% to 34% margin, was the record broken.

The public thought the 1903-05 recession (called the "Rich Man's Panic") wasn't Roosevelt's fault. The problem was that the economic recovery was out-pacing gold currency growth – the 1890s gold inflationary effect was slowing down to the point where the tightening money supply was felt on Wall Street. Fearing a downturn and Roosevelt's pursuit of the trusts, stock prices dropped 26% between July and October 1903. Some New York City banks, caught with their reserves down, failed; business across the country contracted and workers were let go. But all in all it was a sharp recession rather than a major depression. That was to come next.

To remedy the situation, the government pushed up the gold supply (and hence the gold-backed currency) by arranging to transfer gold from European banks. This sparked the economy for another two years but then the British Central Bank (noting that its own economy was sagging as their gold flowed to the US) abruptly raised their interest rate from 3.5% to 6% - a very strong raise. Immediately, investors around the world, including the US, began buying British securities to receive the very generous interest payments. Gold immediately started flowing from the US to England leaving the US currency supply dangerously low. The money supply fell 2.5% from May to September 1907. The effect was first felt on Wall Street in March 1907 when the market crashed and again in October when another market plunge occurred. Overall, the market fell 50% from its 1906 peak. And then the usual effects of a dangerously over-expanded economy subjected to a sudden disturbance started happening: runs on banks, failed banks, a credit crunch, falling production, trade down, businesses closing, workers losing their jobs (8% unemployment in 1908), farm foreclosures rising and consumer demand decreasing.

It was the same old story as we have seen in each economic recession or depression the country had faced, no matter the cause.

One difference in 1908 was the trust companies on Wall Street that acted as banks, taking deposits and making loans. Because they weren't called banks, they had no Federal regulation concerning reserves. Consequently some of them had loans backed by securities from shaky companies that were invested in shares of even more speculative companies. It was a house of cards just waiting to fall down. On October 21, 1907, it did when a regular bank, not especially liking trusts for their non-conservative banking methods, refused checks from the Knickerbocker Trust and a trust run began. Without adequate reserves in the first place, Knickerbocker went under, followed by other trusts and shaky banks.

J. P. Morgan got a lot of press by rounding up a pool of bankers that pledged $25 million in support of falling stocks. His US Steel Company also purchased one shaky company outright for $30 million to stop a domino effect of failing companies. Even the US Treasury pledged $35 million to stabilize the financial system. Still, even though the sharp drop in the market and the trust and bank runs were over by November, the nationwide depression lingered until 1909, not to mention the economic misery of those who lost their jobs and dreams because of some irresponsible "entrepreneurs" on Wall Street trying to maximize profits for themselves. Again, this was the same old scenario of every recession or depression: the "haves" acting greedy in an expansion economy leaving the "have-nots" to pick up the pieces when the bubble explodes.

Another major difference of the 1907-09 depression was the fact that since 1900 when the US went on a singular gold standard without any inflationary effect of silver, it was the first US depression caused by a deficiency in the gold supply. The populist People's Party and the Democrats were right that gold, when not in sufficient supply to back gold dollars, constricts economic growth, indeed even causing recessions or depressions. A less-than-adequate gold supply or even an abundant supply was not something the Federal government could control. It was entirely outside of the hands of the government when the newly discovered gold supplies of the late 1890s picked up the depressed American economy in 1897 and gave it a ride upwards until it faltered in 1903-05 and then crashed in 1907-09. Just as it was outside their hands in 1907 when England raised its interest rates to restore their dwindling gold stocks thereby drawing the gold from America.

What was in the government's hands, however, was the oversight and enforcement of banking regulations that may have averted a crash. It is ridiculous to think that companies taking deposits and lending out that money in speculative ventures can escape such oversight and regulations merely by calling themselves trusts rather than banks. In that regard, the Feds enabled the 1907 crash just as they did in all the silver-affected crashes of the 19th Century.

Federal Reserve System (1913) Even though the 1908 Presidential election occurred in the middle of the 1907-09 depression, Theodore Roosevelt's immense popularity at the time (he was said to have been more popular than even Washington, Jefferson or Lincoln in their prime), insured the victory of William Howard Taft, TR's handpicked successor. But when he and Taft fell out over what Roosevelt considered was a timid pursuit of the trusts by Taft, the public started to cool towards the Republicans. The Democrats winning the Congress in the mid-term 1910 election (for the first time in 16 years) evidenced this. The Democrats have never been Wall Street's (nor corporations') favorite political party – too much representing the little voters as Andrew Jackson, the icon of the Democrats, did. So the Democrats sweeping victory in November 1910 made Wall Street wary. The Supreme Court's decision in March 1911 approving a corporate tax made them even more wary as did the Supreme Court decision on May 15, 1911 ordering the dissolution of the Standard Oil Trust. By summer the stock market was falling. A Federal lawsuit against US Steel triggered a panic and a one-year recession began.

That was enough for the public. Most wanted reform, splitting their votes between the still popular Theodore Roosevelt's

Progressive Republican Party (the Bull Moose party) and Woodrow Wilson's Democratic Party instead of Taft in the 1912 election. Wilson squeaked through with only 42% of the vote.

Tired of the economic roller coaster ride through the 19th Century and now starting another such ride in 1904, 1907 and 1911, all blamed on the plutocrats of banking, corporate trusts and Wall Street, the Democrats (in1913) quickly went to work passing reform acts such as the Federal Reserve Act creating a central bank and branches "to furnish an elastic currency." A graduated income tax in 1914 to "soak the rich" plutocrats followed. These two reforms were two of many the populist People's Party had proposed some twenty years earlier. In a democracy, new ideas, unsettling to many, take years to pass through the system before becoming reality. Women's Suffrage, for example, took some 70 years.

The country didn't have a central bank since 1836 when another Democrat (Andrew Jackson) allowed its charter to expire. Thomas Jefferson, still another Democrat, didn't like Alexander Hamilton's idea of a strong central bank because he feared it would become too dominant and powerful in the nation's finances just as England's Central Bank controlled Britain. Ironically, it was the strength of the English bank in riding out the financial turmoil of 1907-08 that so impressed a visiting Democratic delegation that they convinced their party of the need for a strong central US bank just as the Populists had wanted decades earlier.

The mandate of the Reserve system was to provide economic stability by accommodating commerce and agriculture in their need for operational credit. This was especially true for farmers as the Democrats saw it because it was the farmers who always took the brunt of suffering in an economic downturn. In a downturn, big city banks looked out for themselves, preserving their reserves by denying loans they found risky such as to rural banks who hoped to accommodate the farmers, with a stable source of credit especially during sowing and harvesting time.

Apparently to stop any anguished outcries of bank "nationalization" by the banking industry, the Reserve Act allowed member banks to create, buy shares in, and own the Federal Reserve System while the Federal government would oversee it. Fifteen (later 12) regional banks would serve to accommodate business and agriculture while a Reserve Board, based in Washington D.C. would be the overseer. Nine of the twelve regional banks would have governors appointed by member banks, three by the Board. The Board was comprised of seven members, five appointed by the President and approved by the Senate. The Secretary of the Treasury and the Comptroller of the Currency were the other two members but were later dropped.

Everything looked good on paper to prevent further financial crises but the Board with its political appointees was open to political partisanship. Equally potentially a problem was that there was no economic expertise required to be a member of the Board. Friends of the President could be appointed (and some were). For example, in the 1920s, the Board consisted of a friend, a farmer, a merchant, a newspaper editor and a professor. Adding to potential problems was a conservative/liberal split on Board policy making firm policy decisions on direction difficult.

There is no doubt that the passing of the Federal Reserve Act in 1913 was the most profound economic act that ever made its way through Congress. Little did they know at the time, though, that the law would help lead to the deepest depression the country has ever endured.

It can also be said that the Income Tax Act of 1914 was an equally profound act. It, too, seemed to have a bright future fairly taxing individual's income in a graduated manner. But here too, there were future potential problems in that it gave politicians another means of ingratiating themselves with the voter to win elections. For an economically naïve populace, it could have dire results and did in the decades ahead.

Chapter Three

World War I Expansion/1920-1921 Depression

For some months prior to the start of World War I in the summer of 1914, such European countries as Germany, France and Russia had been stockpiling gold in anticipation of a possible war. Much of the gold had come from the US. That tightened the money supply and slowed down the US economy beginning in 1913. When war did break out, panicky sellers from Europe deluged the London and New York stock markets with sell orders at any price. The markets were forced to close down on July 31. Trade between Europe and the US collapsed, credit froze, banks stopped lending and the other usual calamities occurred. The 1913 slowdown, because of the gold drain, suddenly became a recession in 1914 and lasted until 1915.

Then the gold flow reversed. A deluge of European orders wanting to buy munitions, weapons, commodities and food supplies descended upon the US in 1915. Factories began to hum; workers were hired and economic activity increased across the board. Currency in circulation surged as the increasing gold stocks allowed more printing and minting of money. At the same time, the new Federal Reserve Act had dictated the lowering of Reserve bank reserves from 25% to 18% on demand deposits. This freed up millions for additional lending. The Fed further added to the money expansion by following England's Central Bank's lead in encouraging its citizens to buy war bonds. In each of the four bond drives in the US, the Federal Reserve Board approved open market purchases (OMP) of government securities by the Reserve banks. When paying for these purchases, the securities were paid for with checks on themselves, which eventually ended up back in their banks as deposits. They now had more reserves as well as the securities. It was essentially like printing new money. In this manner the Fed increased credit and economic activity. In such an atmosphere of good times citizens were more likely to buy large amounts of war bonds, which they did.

The United States entered the war in April 1917 producing an increase in the production of war goods that continued the economic expansion during the war. When the war ended a year and a half later in November 1918, there were fears in business, finance and political sectors that a recession would be forthcoming just as every war's end had produced in the past. War goods production was sharply curtailed, business slowed down, workers were laid off and commodity prices plunged. Adding to the anxiety was the employment problem facing the nation when thousands of troops returned from Europe.

Unexpectedly, however, Europe began a flood of orders for manufactured goods to go along with food and raw materials early in 1919. To fulfill these orders, credit grew, business expanded and workers were hired. The money supply increased by $534 million. A boom was on and the stock market led the way, peaking in November 1919. As the demand for them increased, raw materials and commodity prices rose. Demand for workers drove up wages with consumer prices following. As the boom proceeded, inflation increased raising production but reducing the value of money. Rising inflation raised commercial interest rates in early 1920 to 7%, then 8% later in the year.

Benjamin Strong, the governor of the New York Reserve Bank (the dominant Reserve Bank is located in the heart of the financial district) began to worry about the surging market and the rising prices and wages caused by inflation in the later summer of 1919. He proposed to the Federal Reserve Board that the Fed discount rate (rate at which member banks borrow from the Fed) be raised above the long-held 4% to calm the economy. With commercial rates climbing to 7%, member banks could borrow from the Fed at 4% and lend to their customers at the higher commercial rate thereby increasing their profits merely because of the low Fed rate. Customers, including brokerage houses, often lent out the funds at even higher rates to speculators thereby fueling the stock market climb. The Reserve Board said "No" to Strong but on November 3, 1919 the New York Reserve Bank raised their discount to 4 1/4%. Stock prices fell immediately and speculators howled, crying that the Fed was authorized to accommodate business credit needs, not deter stock market activity. Carter Glass, a co-author of the Federal Reserve Act and the Democratic Secretary of the Treasury at the time, agreed. He saw the Fed's role as keeping Fed rates stable, not setting them. Some observers thought he might be worried that if rates went too high it would diminish the chances of a Democratic victory in the upcoming 1920 Presidential election. Critics would later maintain that the Fed should have gradually raised interest rates beginning early in 1919 rather than abruptly higher late in the year to calm the expansion, inflation and speculation.

A 4¼% discount rate, however, wasn't enough to contain the boom. The market rebounded soon after the November rise. With Strong on medical leave in 1920 (he had tuberculosis), the Fed Bank raised the rate to 6% in late January 1920 and to 7% on June 1, 1920.

Depression (1920-1921) The 7% discount rate matching the going commercial rate finally stopped the boom, so much so that the country was thrown into a depression. Benjamin Strong, who didn't vote on the extreme raises because of his medical leave, always maintained that a lower raise earlier in 1919 might have eased the booming economy downward. He saw the 7% raise as too high and too late to do much good, causing fear in the financial and investment communities rather than calm.

Inflation ended almost immediately after the 7% rise. Commodity prices plunged worldwide, wages and prices declined rapidly and businesses failed in the thousands. Unemployment in 1921 neared five million and credit became restricted. Banks went under, farm prices dropped, farms were sold at auction and land values collapsed.

It was sudden and it was throughout the country, not just Wall Street or New York banks. Business confidence began to return by the end of 1921 as the government began using such conventional methods as reducing public debt, reducing military and civil personnel and trimming all government expenditures. At that time, it wasn't the policy for government to come to the aid of business or banking in a downturn of the economy. That had been the policy since the beginning of the nation and wasn't to change for another ten years.

This had been the first economic crisis with which the Federal Reserve System had been designed to deal. Its purpose to stabilize the economy and provide needed credit was believed by the country to be in sound hands. But it failed. This assessment was especially evident by the severe criticism heaped on the Federal Reserve Board by the nation's press and by Congress. Investigations were called for. What should have been done was widely discussed and the guilty were punished.

Benjamin Strong took the severe criticism personally. He was a professional banker his whole career and had a great amount of pride. Neither he, nor the Fed Board, ever forgot the criticism and for him it colored his thinking in the years ahead. For one thing, he came to realize that the discount rate was too publicly transparent, a "red flag" bringing fear to the financial community that could affect business and employment adversely. He apparently decided after the experience of the depression that there was another means to stabilize the economy and accommodate business and farmers as the Reserve Act was intended and that was open market purchases or sales – a much more quiet procedure that wouldn't ruffle so many feathers.

The second Presidential term (1917-21) of Woodrow Wilson must have been difficult for him and his Democratic Party. In the election of 1916, he campaigned as the "man who kept us out of the war." Just six months later in April 1917, he had Congress declare war on Germany. A year and a half later, during which the economy boomed with war production and patriotic war bond drives, in the mid-term 1918 election, just a week before the Armistice that ended a victorious war, the voters repudiated Wilson and the Democrats by electing a Republican Congress. One has to wonder if such a major political defeat was more about Wilson not keeping his implied promise to the country in 1916 to continue to keep the country out of war than for any other reason, such as Theodore Roosevelt's opposition to the Fourteen Points Peace Plan of Wilson's.

With Congress in Republican hands, almost automatically dooming any Senate ratification of Wilson's peace treaty incorporating a League of Nations, he toured the country in the summer of 1919 trying to drum up popular support for the treaty. In September, he suffered a stroke that incapacitated him for the rest of his term.

If that wasn't enough hardship for him, the country's inflationary expansion during the war brought soaring prices and millions of worker going on strike for wage increases to keep up with the prices. This turned the public against the unions. There were also anarchists' bombings, a communist "red scare," the revival of the Ku Klux Klan, Negro lynching in the south, and race riots in the north. Overall, it was a socially turbulent time, all on the Democratic watch.

The topper, of course, was the rapid plunge into the depression in 1920 as a result of the Reserve Board's approval of a discount rate rise to 7%. One has to question the timing of the Board's raising the discount rate in the spring of 1920 just five months before the fall election. Presumably, the majority of the Board members leaned toward the Democrats, as they were Wilson appointees. But such a steep rise was definitely to the Republican's advantage. Was the pressure from the governors of the regional banks too much for the Board's Democrats to overcome? If so, the fears at the outset of the Reserve System in 1913 that it could easily become politically partisan were possibly fulfilled. What had started out in 1916 as a happy time for the Democrats ended in a shambles in 1920. And as always, the party associated in the voters' mind with an economic disaster has always been voted out of office at the next election.

Chapter Four

1920s Expansion/1930s Great Depression

And so they were in 1920. The country had had its fill of Democrats and intellectuals in the White House. Warren G. Harding (a backroom compromise candidate) and Calvin Coolidge easily defeated the Democrats James M. Cox and Franklin D. Roosevelt by a record amount at that time of 61% to 34% of the total vote. One of Harding's first appointments was that of his friend from his hometown in Ohio, D. R. Crissinger, as Federal Reserve Board Chairman. The financial community and the Secretary of the Treasury protested but Harding had his way. According to Benjamin Anderson in his excellent book *Economics and the Public Welfare* (1949, Van Nostrand Co., Princeton, NJ, p. 117) the appointment was political with the sole purpose of re-electing Harding and other Republicans.

Because of Crissinger's inexperience (he was neither an economist nor a banker), Benjamin Strong (the Governor of the New York Reserve Bank) now became the dominant force in the system even though he wasn't on the Board. Crissinger's appointment had denied him that plumb. If Franklin D. Roosevelt was the story of the 1930s depression, then Benjamin Strong was the story behind the 1920s expansion. He was over six feet tall, wiry, imposing, strong willed, purposeful. Other bankers recognized him for his excellent administrative abilities, organization and planning skills. Pragmatic rather than intellective, he had been a trust bank president in New York when the appointed governors of the Reserve Banks asked him to be the governor of the New York Reserve Bank, the so-called jewel in the system. Hesitant at first, he didn't trust politicians, especially Democrats and their restrictive Federal Reserve Act. Being a lifelong Republican he also didn't want to be a part of a Democrat program. Republican banker friends convinced him, however, to accept the post as being in a strong position to direct policy (Chandler, 1978).

For a purposeful man with visionary ideas, his greatest asset would prove to be his charming, persuasive manner in bringing around colleagues (especially Reserve Board members) to his way of thinking. At social gatherings, he was especially effective. In modern parlance he sounds as if he was a schmoozer par excellence.

Not all observers, however, admired his abilities or his ideas. To some critics he was a shortsighted, inept, unconventional banker without any knowledge of economic theory. To them, his ideas directing Board policy were dangerous to the economy. Unfortunately for the country, they would be proven right.

Perhaps his biggest critic was Adolph Miller, the academic economist of the Board who considered Strong overly aggressive and a usurper of power. Miller would usually take the opposite stance to Strong. Disliking obstructionist views to his own, Strong considered Miller an overly verbose, pompous, typical stuffed-shirt college academic.

Strong had been very upset in September 1919 when his request to allow his New York Reserve Bank to raise the discount rate to calm the incipient economic boom was refused by the Board. He was angrier when the Board, in his sick-leave absence in 1920, raised the rate to 7% in June 1920 triggering the depression. The severe criticism of the Board's policy afterwards hurt him personally. The millions of workers put out of work because of that Board decision (which he considered too late) made him vow that it wouldn't happen again if he could help it.

If the Federal Reserve Act's purpose was to stabilize the economy and accommodate timely credit for business and farming, he believed the less obvious way to do it was with the purchase or sale of securities on the open market. He would get the Fed to purchase the securities whenever the economy was sagging – paying for the securities with Federal money which put money into the economy, increased credit and stimulated the economy. If the economy started to boom, he would sell open market securities thus sucking money out of the system, decreasing credit and slowing down the economy. He could envision taking out the ups and downs, leveling out the economy to provide long-range stability as well as always-available credit. And there wouldn't be any jobs lost nor economic misery for the country. It would be a planned, proactive policy and not an emergency, reactive one.

Wishing to aid the recovery from the 1920-21 depression, Strong set up an open market committee in the New York Reserve Bank in early 1922 and became its de facto chairman. By June of the same year, the Reserve banks, especially the New York bank, had purchased a half billion dollars worth of government securities on the open market. This stimulated the economy as planned, producing a period of expansion with easy money and credit. Also beginning in 1921 and extending into 1922, nearly a billion dollars worth of gold had flowed in mostly from Europe in the form of war-loan payments and post-war purchase payments. This added greatly to the expansive atmosphere in 1922, a mid-term election.

Three months after the November election that the Republicans won, Strong's open market committee not only sold securities but also raised the discount rate from 4 to 4 1/3%. Both acts calmed the robust activity that took place before the election. Anderson (ibid., p. 135), as a conservative banker, thought that the Fed had not been created to produce easy money and credit "lightheartedly." He found it irresponsible and warned of future dire results if it continued. Still, the Fed continued buying before elections and selling afterwards throughout the 1920s.

To be fair, the Fed activity in buying and selling securities could just as well be construed as Strong's plan in action – getting the country out of the depression by expansion and then contracting the economy to keep it from getting overheated, returning it to stability. Any timing with elections might very well be merely coincidental. When asked about the open market purchase activity, the standard Fed answer was that it increased member bank reserves and provided security interest payments to cover expenses.

Even though the Reserve Board in Washington, DC demanded control of the open market committee that Strong had started in the New York Reserve Bank, he was still able to instigate the buying and selling of securities when he deemed it necessary. In fact, through most of 1924 almost up to the time of the Presidential election, the Fed was again buying open market securities ostensibly to pull the economy out of another down period (late 1923, early 1924). Close to $500 million were purchased. And once again, as soon as the election was over, securities were sold, draining money and credit from the economy, slowing it down. Strong may have been fine-tuning the economy again. If so, his methods were apparently successful as prosperity continued. Calvin Coolidge won big against the Democrat John Davis and the Progressive Robert LaFollette in 1924. Coolidge was all for economy and after that "more economy." H. L.

Mencken (1880-1956), the cantankerous journalist, thought Coolidge was for the "Haves" and LaFollette for the "Have Nots."

The economy leveled out through most of 1925, still prosperous with more than adequate credit suggesting that Strong's tweaking of the economy was working. Still, during most of 1926, the Fed Board approved another round of security purchasing of around $150 million before the mid-term election (1926) that the Republicans again won on continuing prosperity.

Another economic contraction period starting shortly after the 1926 election brought forth another Board approval of a Strong initiative to purchase eventually a total of $200 million of open market securities. The discount rate was also reduced from 4 to 3½% in the summer of 1927 to further stimulate the economy as well as to aid Britain to accumulate gold to maintain its gold supply. Gold flowed into countries with higher interest rates attractive to investors.

The new 3½% US rate, however, had an immediate psychological impetus on the stock market – the Dow Jones average doubled in just six months. Heretofore, the average had slowly risen along with the nation's business earnings since 1922. Now suddenly the DJ average surged upwards leaving the earnings curve behind.

Both curves from 1922 to the summer of 1927 were, of course, propped up by Strong's periodical "stimulus packages" (1922, '24, '26 and '27). More money in the consumers' pockets meant that more autos, radios, refrigerators, etc. were sold resulting in always-rising earnings and related stock prices. Indeed, it can be argued that without the Fed's continuous largesse, there probably wouldn't have been a Roaring Twenties period (nor a stock market crash/depression).

Strong was always irritated by market speculation thwarting his economic balancing act and the doubling of the market during late 1927 was no exception. In early 1928, he had to contract the economy to rein in the market. By June 1928, the Board had sold $300 million in securities and $100 million in bills to take money out of the system. It had also raised the discount rate back to 4%; by July, it was 5%. This had disastrous effects in Europe, especially Germany. Investment money and gold started flowing back to the US. Europe, to keep its remaining gold, had to raise its interest rates. This constricted their economies, again especially in Germany which was heavily in debt to foreign lenders and had war reparations to pay. German and European unemployment began to rise resulting in recession and later (in 1930) depression.

The Fed's attempts to cool the stock market throughout 1928 and early 1929 didn't stop the market but they did slow down business. Automobile and steel production declined. The Republican high farm tariff in 1921 had impacted farm prices and prosperity negatively throughout the 1920s. By 1928 the stock market had taken on a life of its own. It no longer had to depend on the Fed Board's largesse. As demand for loans to buy market shares increased with each Fed expansion period, the commercial loan rates rose so that by 1927 they were 4% while the Fed rate was 3½%. By the end of 1928, they were 6½% to the Fed's 5% and 8% in 1929 to the Fed's 5%. Before the October 1929 crash, the commercial rate reached 10 or 12% to the Fed's 5%. The New York Reserve Bank wanted permission to raise their rate to 6% in early 1929 but was refused by the Board.

It was the beginning of the end when commercial loan rates surpassed the Fed rate. It meant that banks and brokerages could make money just by borrowing low at the Reserve banks and lending high to customers, usually speculators willing to pay 10 or 12% for a loan to buy stocks because their stocks were going up so fast.

To make matters worse in 1929, the high rates on call loans for stock purchases attracted huge sums of money from trusts, corporations and foreigners eager to take advantage of the high rates. After the 1929 crash, it was estimated that the call loans amounted to nearly $9 billion by 1929 and that three quarters of the loans came from this "outside" money. So even though the Fed Board sold some $400 million in securities and $200 million in bills through 1928 and the first half of 1929 to restrict money and credit, the market no longer heeded Fed actions. In fact, the "outside" money was negating all the Fed efforts to cool the market. Besides that, the Fed, after a year and a half of selling, was running out of securities to sell.

Benjamin Strong's tubercular symptoms were getting worse each year. In September 1926 he became ill in Europe, returned home and took sick leave until the spring of 1927. Then, starting in early 1928, his condition worsened. He died in October of that year at the age of 56.

Without Strong as a decisive leader for the system and the Board, there was no agreed upon policy to constrict the soaring market without restricting credit to business and farming. The Fed Board debated as to whether they had any authority to interfere with the market, whether to raise margin rates. Early on a stock could be bought for ten cents on the dollar – a 10% margin rate. Later on in 1929, increasingly cautious brokerages demanded a 45-50% margin in cash to buy stock. With some speculators seeing a 500% rise in their stock prices, a high margin rate wasn't a problem.

Although the New York Reserve Bank (Strong's old bank) had wanted to raise the discount rate to match the commercial rate, the Board members didn't want the responsibility for triggering a market crash and ensuing depression as had happened in 1920-21 when they raised the discount rate. Instead, the now-timid Board wanted to use "moral persuasion" to limit bank loans to speculators. But once the "outside" money was more expansive than the Fed's contraction efforts, it was only a matter of time.

The Crash of 1929 Notwithstanding what has been called a sense of euphoria on Wall Street in 1928-29; there was most likely a sense of nervousness in big players. The times were too good to last and they knew it but their avariciousness kept them in the game. If the big crash came, they were ready to bolt but until that time, like a gambler on a hot streak, they couldn't take their bets off the table. Still, their nervousness was reflected in the fitful surges and plunges the market took in 1928 and early 1929. After Hoover won in November 1928, the market surged; in December, it plunged. If the speculator sensed the big crash was coming, he would sell and retire to another room and count his winnings. If the crash didn't come, he would buy right back in riding the after-plunge surge. When the Fed board met in Washington towards the end of March 1929 in daily session for a week without any statements for the press, the market plunged sure that the Fed was going to do something drastic to halt the market. When nothing drastic happened, the market, with the help of a New York bank willing to lend money to support the market, surged upwards and continued to climb.

Except to raise the discount rate to 6% in August 1929, The Fed Board appeared to distance itself from the irrational exuberance of Wall Street hoping in so doing to also distance itself from the responsibility for the collapse when eventually it would come.

As spring passed into summer in 1929, the stock market frenzy actually increased. Broker-to-customer loans increased each summer month averaging $400 million a month with September the highest month of all at $650 million. By October 1929, total broker loans stood at $9.1 billion.

The frenzy extended throughout the country. Lore had it that every little guy in the country – plumbers, clerks, shopkeepers, even housewives – were putting their hard-earned cash in the market. Actually the real numbers were probably closer to several million. After reading the headlines every day about another market rise, the lure of a "sure thing" finally got to them in 1928-29 and they made the leap especially into investment trusts (the most shaky vehicles for investing as it turned out).

Unfortunately, by hesitating for several years, when they finally did decide to buy, it was invariably at the top of the market.

Everyone wanted to get rich. Some by any means whatsoever. There were the unscrupulous newspapermen who (for a large fee) would tout a specific stock in their articles or columns.

Also, dishonest specialists on the trading floor of the stock exchanges would pool their money and buy one specialist's stock. Because it was the specialist's job to set the price for the stock he handled depending on the buy and sell orders, it was easy for him to quietly nudge up the stock price every day to the point where a good profit was had by all in the pool when the stock was sold.

This "nudging up" was also done by individual specialists for a stock in their own portfolio, the content of which was used daily in setting the price of the stock. Indeed, this practice has always been considered a "perk" ever since stock exchanges were devised. As long as the specialist set the price, it was easy to get away with it. In the computer age, critics of this perk have advocated the setting of stock prices by computers. The specialists, of course, have fought the innovation tooth and nail.

At the other end of the scam spectrum was the "friendly" insurance agent handling the insurance proceeds for a recently bereaved widow. He would talk her into doubling or even tripling her paltry funds (usually around $2000, a standard insurance policy of the day). If she hesitated, citing her investment ignorance, he would reassure her that he knew an "honest" broker who would "do right by her." When she turned over the money to the broker, he would give a kickback to the "friendly" insurance agent and then charge the widow an inflated commission to cover the kickback and his own commission. The poor widow would lose upwards of 25% of her dead husband's insurance money before a stock was even purchased. Of course, when the crash came all the little investors were the first to lose their money and probably "honest" brokers as well.

The market faltered the week after Labor Day. John K. Galbraith, in his marvelous book written in his best sardonic style (*The Great Crash, 1929,* Houghton Mifflin, Boston, 1988, p. 84), believed that the soaring market reached its peak on September 3; thereafter into the October collapse, it was a downward market.

Maybe some savvy investors who were worried about the downward industrial production figures all summer long got out of the market. But those endowed with an exaggerated sense of optimism appeared to stay in the game as the record high broker loans for September testify. Perhaps the lure of bargains was their main motivation.

Contrary to public lore, the big collapse wasn't confined to one day in October. The initial break started on a Saturday morning, October 19. After a weekend wondering what to do, many seem to have decided to play it safe, take their profits and not be too greedy. The selling started slowly on Monday, picked up speed by Wednesday and accelerated on Thursday morning the 24th – Black Thursday. Even the overly optimistic speculators were getting out now or being sold out by nervous brokerage houses making margin calls to get more cash to cover the losses in the collateral stock they had for call loans. Those cautious brokers who had started to demand 45-50% margin for a call loan must have felt a lot better than those who required only 10%.

But that would be short lived. The next week brought the worst plunge of all – Black Tuesday, October 29th. If anyone still thought that this was a merely a correction in the market, they must have been in the minority. The big problem was, as the stock prices dropped, speculators couldn't come up with the extra cash that the margin calls were demanding. Consequently, the brokers were forced to sell the collateral stock at the best price they could get and this comprised most of the millions of shares being sold, driving the market down still further.

By mid November, the bloodletting calmed a bit. One can only imagine the state of shock Wall Street and the country felt. Billions had been lost, especially by the wealthy investors and the banking community. What to do? Some thought the damage as of

November 13, 1929 wasn't too catastrophic. For example, the *New York Times* industrial index of economic activity, which had been 449, the last of August was 224 after the havoc, 50% lower (Galbraith, ibid.). Most stocks had lost an equal amount. Recovery seemed possible but how and when?

The Great Depression 1930-1941 As the new decade started, the Federal Reserve System found itself without a persuasive leader. Since Benjamin Strong's death in October 1928, the Board had no firm policy in dealing with the then pending crash nor afterwards. It was divided, indecisive and at times deadlocked between liberal elements wanting a strong proactive policy to the emergency and conservative elements wanting a more conventional banking approach of letting the needed adjustments take place naturally. The Hoover administration favored the latter hands-off approach allowing business to recover on its own. The government would help by balancing the budget and providing a sound money policy backed by the traditional gold standard. It had worked in 1907. "Prosperity is just around the corner" was their mantra.

It was Strong's New York Reserve Bank that pushed for active measures. It had lowered its discount rate to 5% during the crash days and had started purchasing open market securities at the same time providing easier money and credit to lower interest rates and make recovery loans more feasible.

President Hoover declared a token tax cut of one percent in November 1929 and chaired several meetings in December with leading banking and business leaders in which he urged them to keep up capital investment and maintain their payrolls. His actions appeared to be more for public confidence than to come to grips with the actual problems. Privately he and his advisors worried about the possible speculation and inflation that they believed the Federal Reserve Board's renewed policy of open market purchases would produce in the form of easy money and credit. It was just such policies they believed that caused the market crash in the first place.

Consequently, by December, the Reserve Board was apparently asked to end the renewed open-market securities purchases. Still, the stock market took note of the Fed's purchases; it rallied from January to March 1930 and then fell gradually.

Business, on the other hand, continued on its own downward trend. This can be seen in the unemployment figures: in 1929 before the crash, unemployment stood at 3% of the labor force; in the autumn of 1930, just a year later, it had risen to 9% (Amity Shlaes, *The Forgotten Man,* 2007, Harper Collins, New York).

The cheap money and credit policy of the Federal Reserve Board from late October to December 1929 seemed to have had no impact on business at all. Many businessmen and their companies had been heavily involved in the market either through stock purchases or call loan money and had lost thousands if not millions in the crash. They were in no mood to borrow or expand. They, like the banks, were trying to preserve their cash; any income they made went towards paying off personal or company loans as protection against any future upheavals. Those who didn't have adequate income were going bankrupt. To stay afloat, businesses were cutting hours and wages, laying off workers, shutting down branch factories or even selling out if they could find buyers.

With thousands of workers being laid off, consumer demand was dropping fast as was the country's productivity. Everyone was trying to preserve cash to weather out the storm. They hoarded gold coins and bills just as the banks were doing. Soon they would be forced to take out their remaining cash in droves from banks all over the country as the downward spiral was picking up speed.

The farmer's plight was even worse. All during the 1920s, low crop prices due to Republican high farm tariffs that brought retaliatory foreign tariffs kept the farmers from exporting their surplus crops. The result was a dumping on the domestic market of the surplus keeping prices perpetually low. The Republicans urged farmers to plant more each year to make up for lost profits the previous year, which just increased the surplus on the domestic market each year. As 1930 began, the rising unemployment cut back on people buying even necessary food. This further deepened the farmers' plight.

Economists, in later years, would look back on the year 1930 as the pivotal year between the 1929 crash and the impending depression of the later years. They later thought that if the Feds, both the government and the Reserve System, had had an easy money and credit policy during 1930, the eventual depression might have been stopped at the outset replaced, perhaps, by a severe recession. But instead of loosening the money and credit supply that fateful year, the official policy was one of tightening the supply.

In the gathering economic gloom of early 1930, the Republican Congress passed the Hawley-Smoot Tariff Bill in June. Benjamin Anderson (ibid. p. 224), a banker, economist, professor and author, called it the worst "folly" of the government between 1929 and 1933. In an unprecedented move, 1028 economists took out a full-page ad in *The New York Times* urging Hoover to veto the extremely high tariff bill that they said would destroy foreign trade and cause worldwide unemployment.

Hoover, however, being a true Republican with their obsessive liking of high tariffs to keep out cheap foreign goods as a means of preserving American jobs, signed the bill. Almost immediately other countries around the world (especially Europe, our biggest export customer), raised high tariff walls in retaliation; world trade almost came to a stand still.

The United States had been averaging nearly $1.5 billion a year since 1913 in export-import trade (Shlaes, ibid.). In a country spiraling into an economic depression in which it could use desperately all the economic activity, profits and jobs it could get it seems ludicrous that the Republicans would deny some $1.5 billion to the economy. Anderson (ibid.) had noted that many of the Republican Senators and Representatives elected in the 1920 Republican landslide were ignorant in economics. Presumably many of those members were still present in Congress in 1930.

Export industry jobs worldwide evaporated along with trade. US farm prices already declining in 1930 accelerated downward, the rest of the year after the tariff bill was signed. Even the stock market took a nosedive the following week. Economic activity was dropping so low that even a very low 2% Fed discount rate by the end of the year had no effect in stimulating the economy.

By fall, the tariff had decreased farm prices to the point where farmers could no longer repay their seeding and harvesting loans to the rural banks. The banks, in turn, were finding it increasingly difficult to borrow from the big city banks to maintain their reserves because the urban banks were reserving their own capital, looking askance at any loans they considered risky. Banks, mostly rural, started failing in October 1930 and by the end of the year over 600 banks had failed.

With the headlines reporting more banks failing each week, depositors started to worry about the safety of their deposits in their own banks and withdrawals increased dramatically. This was especially true for the New York bank The Bank of the United

States. Conservative banks in New York had always been wary of it even opposing its name when originally chartered, maintaining that the imposing name was meant to mislead Jewish immigrants into thinking that it was the official bank of the United States. It had also dealt heavily in second and third mortgages during the booming 1920s when money and credit were plentiful. But now that money was tight, those loans were going into default. With withdrawals increasing all over the country, The Bank of the United States was no exception. It found itself cash poor. When the word got out, the withdrawals turned into a run and the bank had to turn to other New York banks for help. Merger attempts were made but when the potential new owners saw the bank's books, they shied away. On December 11, 1930 the bank failed, the largest bank in the country yet to fail. The failure was controversial because some reports said the bank's books were in good order. Others said the New York banks' failure to protect it was an anti-Semitic action because of all the Jewish depositors the bank had. In any case, those depositors were outraged when the other banks guaranteed only 50% of the remaining deposits.

Neither the other New York banks nor apparently the Federal Reserve Board thought the Bank of the United States was significant enough to save. But they badly misread the country's fears. When news of the failure of the "official" Bank of the United States spread around the country, more bank runs and failures ensued.

Under pressure from Congress "to do something," the Reserve Board reluctantly resumed purchasing of open market securities in early 1931. The stock market again responded a bit as it did in January-March of 1930 but ran out of steam in the spring. Business, however, still declined, as did the country's productivity. Unemployment reached 17.4% in September 1931 (Shlaes, ibid.) nearly double from a year ago.

More woe was soon to follow. The fallout from the horrendous Hawley-Smoot Tariff of June 1930, which had first devastated American farm prices leading to rural bank failures that autumn and eventually to The Bank of the United States failure in early December, not only spread fear of bank solvency in the United States but also in Europe. Germany was especially hard hit by falloff in international trade after the tariff. It had relied on that trade to bring in foreign currency, which they then redeemed into gold to pay off their war reparations, especially to France. They already had some five million jobless at the start of 1931. The fall off of trade only added to the number as export workers were laid off. Increasingly, unemployed communist workers clashed in the streets with jobless nationalistic workers. The country was in social turmoil as well as financial turmoil as the economy descended into depression.

As a desperate measure in order to keep their factories open and regain some foreign currency to pay their debts, the Germans entered into a trade agreement with neighboring Austria. The French objected strongly calling the agreement an annexation plan to strengthen Germany beyond what the war peace treaty allowed. France quickly redeemed their Austrian currency holdings for Austrian gold. Other countries followed suit draining Austria's gold supply leading to the failure of a leading Austrian bank on May 29, 1931 and eventually the collapse of their financial system, abandoning the gold standard.

Just as in the states the previous fall, when the collapse of US banks led to widespread fear for the safety of depositors' money and triggered further runs on banks, the same thing happened in Europe. The run on German banks started June 1, 1931 and continued during the summer until its financial system was in a shambles. After Germany, fearful that England having financial problems might also go off the gold standard and devalue the sterling holdings of other countries, prompted the countries to redeem their holdings in English gold. England, already weak in gold holdings, couldn't withstand the gold drain and abandoned the standard. France followed on September 20, 1931. A week later, Sweden and Norway also abandoned the standard (Anderson, ibid.).

Fearful that the US mired in depression might be the next country to go off the gold standard, a foreign run on American gold started soon after England had thrown in the towel. In just two days the US lost $118 million in gold as the foreign countries redeemed their dollar holdings before they might be devalued. By the end of 1931, another $400 million flowed out.

Soon the foreign fear about their dollar holdings spread to the US depositors. A second surge of US bank runs began in the summer of 1931. By January 1932, nearly 2000 more banks had failed. Bank deposits fell $5.7 billion in the last quarter of 1931. Money and credit became even tighter as the gold flowed out and the deposits dropped. To make matters worse, tax revenues as of

June 30 showed an $800 million drop from the year before. To offset the tightening of the money supply due to the gold loss, the Reserve Board was forced to put $1.1 billion into the economy by purchasing securities. But the nation was in shock; the banks couldn't be trusted nor the Federal Reserve System nor the Hoover/Republican government. More Fed purchases were too little and too late. Everything was going down – the stock market, production, prices, income, tax revenues – the only thing constantly going up was unemployment.

The foreign gold run continued during the first half of 1932 as did the US bank failures. To shore up the banks, Hoover was forced to change the government's hands-off policy and signed the proactive Reconstruction Finance Corporation Bill on January 22, 1932. This was designed to provide loans to struggling banks. At the same time (February 27, 1932) he signed an Act which allowed for government securities to act as collateral for Federal Reserve notes which eased the money and credit situation. Congressional pressure also forced the Fed Board to purchase another one billion dollars in government securities. They stopped purchasing when Congress adjourned in the summer of 1932 even though the sagging stock market perked up that summer (as did farm prices and industrial production). If the security purchases had continued, the economy might have finally started upwards.

Mr. Hoover, however, wasn't finished with tightening the money supply. In 1932, he signed a bill raising the income tax. The top rate on incomes over $500,000 had been in the mid 20%; he raised it to 63%. The top rate when the income tax started in 1914 had been 7% (Shlaes, ibid.).

The people who earned such high incomes were also the same people who supplied jobs. In a country needing jobs, it didn't make much sense to impede job formation. But with dropping Federal tax revenue each year, that old Republican dogma that balancing the budget in down times was the way to good times probably convinced Hoover it was a correct move. If only the country would be patient, "prosperity was just around the corner."

The Democrats, too, weren't innocent in impeding the recovery during these fateful years. When suspicions arose that the Reconstruction Finance Corporation was using favoritism in giving loans to banks, the Democratically controlled House demanded that the list of banks receiving loans be made public. When it was (first on August 22, 1932 and again on January 6,

1933), depositors who saw their bank on the list didn't hesitate to quickly withdraw their money from what was officially listed as a troubled bank (Anderson, ibid.). Whether the Democrats knew their actions would cause bank runs isn't known but in an election year, all seems to be fair if not quite ethical.

Franklin Delano Roosevelt It shouldn't have been any question as to who would win the November 1932 Presidential election. One candidate was a conservative, staid, uninspiring introvert who the people no longer listened to and the other was a liberal, optimistic, inspiring extrovert who spoke of action and change. FDR won handily by some seven million votes. The people loved him. The wealthy disliked him and feared what he would do to the nation's business.

Although FDR preached hope to the masses, he practiced hate for the upper class. Like all true demagogues, he played on the people's passions and prejudices to obtain power and control. And like all demagogues, he needed villains to rail about. Adolph Hitler had the Jews, the humiliating peace treaty and the French; Roosevelt had the bankers, corporate heads and Wall Street. For all his work programs and regulatory agencies designed to pull the country out of the depression as his campaign rhetoric promised, he only succeeded in prolonging the depression. According to Amity Shlaes, (*The Forgotten Man,* ibid.), FDR never was able to get unemployment below double digits, starting at 23% in 1933 and ending at 14.6% in 1940.

Comparing these figures with the unemployment rate of 3.5% before the 1929 crash show that Roosevelt's "alphabet soup" of policies aimed against the rich were not producing needed jobs. Even the 1940 figure after some seven years of trying was more than four times higher than the 1920s figure.

The failure to produce jobs for the little man can be understood very simply. The public, to whom Roosevelt pandered to remain in power and control, did not produce jobs. The rich did whether Roosevelt and his advisors liked it or not. The rich had the money, the connections, and the know how to open factories and hire workers; the public did not.

Ironically, the Bolsheviks, after they had brutally taken over the original Socialist government following the Russian Revolution in 1917, faced the same dilemma as the Roosevelt New Dealers. The Bolsheviks purged the rich only to find that jobs disappeared with the purging. Their state economic planning agency (Gosplan) was never as efficient in creating jobs as the rich had been. Consequently the Soviet system in its early years was plagued by unemployment, poverty and hunger.

One has to assume that an intelligent President and the college professors comprising his "brain trust" of advisors knew this simple, common sense truth. That said, because they failed to produce jobs, one could only assume that their hatred bias against the rich, when coming into office and throughout the 1930s, made them see the rich as villains to be punished and penalized and not as job providers.

The "brain trust" was especially hateful of the rich. As liberal college professors they all possessed the socialistic mindset so favored by the intellectuals of the time starting with the English Fabian Society of the intelligentsia around the turn of the century. To them, there had to be a better way than cold, cruel capitalism or brutal totalitarianism at the other extreme. To the Fabians, socialism was the ideal middle way - profit for the good of society rather than for the individual. With that mindset, it is no wonder that the brain trust wanted to rein in the fat cats, regulate their industries, banks and businesses and raise up labor, insuring them a prosperous and decent life.

The first target of the brain trust's "wrecking crew" was the rich man's gold standard. Populists had long argued that the gold standard restricted economic growth and kept down farm prices. Alan Greenspan, Chairman of the Federal Reserve System (1987-2004) in his book *The Age of Turbulence,* (2007, Penguin Press, New York, p. 481) reports that the gold standard did indeed keep down prices. From 1870-1913, the cost of living rose just two tenths of one percent per year as compared to a 4.5% per year rise from 1939-1989 when the country was off the gold standard. To the New Dealers though, lower prices were the problem. Business wouldn't recover if too low prices wouldn't provide a profit. So to raise prices, the gold standard had to go.

Two things happened before FDR entered office on March 4, 1933, which makes one wonder if the brain trust hadn't concocted a Machiavellian plan to get rid of the gold standard under cover of an emergency banking crisis. First, after the November 1932 election, rumors spread that President-elect Roosevelt was going to dump the gold standard as soon as he entered office in March. Was this a purposeful leak? They must have known the rumors would trigger another foreign gold run as well as a domestic run on banks with depositors this time requesting their money in gold coins and bullion.

To apparently add to the domestic bank run turmoil, the Democratic House once again demanded in January the public disclosure of the names of banks lent money by the Reconstruction Finance Corporation. Their previous demand in August had triggered bank runs so they must have known that a new demand would do the same. This latter Democratic move doesn't make any sense other than a deliberate attempt to create a gold emergency.

By the time Roosevelt entered office on March 4, 1933 almost all the states had declared a bank holiday to keep more banks from failing. It was the perfect cover for the New Dealers to end the gold standard.

When Roosevelt, after entering office, discussed the banking crisis with his New Dealers behind closed doors, it was noticed by bankers countrywide that the Federal Reserve officials were not present at the meeting. This was a clear sign that the new administration would deal with the bank crisis alone and not with the rich man's cronies. Cooperation with the villains of the crash and ensuing depression was not to be the FDR watchword throughout the 1930s.

It is interesting to note that twenty leading economists of the country sent a letter to the President-elect in early January 1933 advising him to remain on the gold standard to accelerate economic recovery. Both party planks in the November election advocated a strong gold standard as did leading Democrats in Congress. Even Roosevelt, in his campaign speeches, promised to stay on the gold standard.

Once the banks were reopened after a few days of closure, Roosevelt, under authority granted by his Democratic Congress, declared on April 5 that the people could no longer own gold coins, bullion or certificates. Although the country was still on the gold standard as FDR had promised, it was going to be a less restrictive, devalued standard.

The next strike against gold was on June 5, 1933 when FDR signed a Congressional resolution eliminating all gold payment clauses in bond and security contracts, both government and private. After all, it was only the rich and well-to-do middle class who held or lent such items. It is estimated that some $200 billion was lost by the rich creditor class with one stroke of FDR's pen (Schlaes, ibid.).

One can only imagine the shock to the wealthier citizens at Roosevelt's first acts in office and one can also see why he was never successful in producing jobs. The Soviet Bolsheviks rounded up the rich and shot them or sent them off to Siberia before confiscating their wealth. Roosevelt and his socialistic brain trust used more "humane" methods by slowly taking their wealth away rather than their lives.

And more was to come in taking wealth from the moneyed classes. First, in the Gold Reserve Act of January 1934, the amount of gold backing the dollar was reduced by almost 41% thereby devaluing the dollar. The new dollar was to have only 59% gold backing. Gold's new price was $35 an ounce compared to the old price of $20.67. To the rich this meant that if they had $100,000 in old dollar assets, they were now worth only $59,000 in buying power if prices remained the same.

A second maneuver to bleed the rich was the Revenue Bill in the summer of 1935, which raised income tax rates especially on the well to do. A $100,000 income was now taxed at 41%; the old rate at 37.7%. If one was really rich with a $5 million income or more, the new rate was 83.8% instead of the old 69.9%.

Both acts weren't conducive to providing new jobs, taking assets away from the very people who could provide new jobs. Even if the government used the new revenue and devalued dollars "profit" in gold to stimulate the economy, the unemployment figures weren't lowered appreciably overall. The timing of the bills before the 1936 election suggests that FDR and the Democratic Congress were "sticking it" to the rich just as they had promised.

A third, and probably most drastic of the pre-election displays of "sticking it," was the Undistributed Profits Tax Act in 1936 which taxed profits retained by a corporation for future expansion. The top rate here was almost 74% which definitely impeded capital investment in undertaking new ventures or in expansion of production facilities. Some conservative Democrats in Congress were successful in limiting the tax to only 27% on corporate retained profits over 68% of their adjusted net income. Roosevelt wasn't very happy with the limitation (Anderson, ibid.).

All three of the pre-election maneuvers must have put some fear and trepidation into the moneyed class, seeing their assets dwindling away because of official government action. Nothing like this had ever happened before. Comparisons to a totalitarian regime were becoming more commonplace among business people and the rich.

The 1936 Election To understand the events leading up to and the eventual results of the 1936 election, it is necessary to understand the psychological motivations of FDR. History describes leading figures in the light of their actions but rarely touches upon the long disappeared inner motives behind those actions. In Roosevelt's case, behind that sparkling smile and ingratiating charm lurked a cunning, vindictive politician willing to do anything to win an election.

Like most politicians, FDR was a born egotist imbued with an innate sense of superiority over his peers. His actions his entire life were to convince others, and especially himself, that his superiority sense was justified. With this trait came a compulsive need to be number one, to win at all things, to display his superiority outwardly and bask (modestly?) in the adulation.

To insure that he indeed would win the 1936 Presidential election, FDR, as we have seen, opened one pre-election front by "sticking it" to the rich which was meant to ingratiate him with the voters. A second front soon followed but not too close to the election as to be too obvious for buying votes.

First, to lock up the elderly vote, the Social Security Act was rolled out in August 1935. Although a very good Act for future retirement funds in a population adverse to saving, it nonetheless put an immediate tax burden on employers and employees. With income in sparse supply in 1935, it would have been more advantageous to economic recovery if it could have been delayed until jobs became more plentiful and income increased. But 1935 was when it was needed in FDR's plans.

The labor vote was locked up earlier that summer with the passage of the Wagner Act on July 5, 1935. This act made unionizing easier as well as getting higher wages. John L. Lewis, the union boss, was said to have been ecstatic over the Wagner Act. His enthusiasm, however, would soon lead to union excesses in the years ahead.

Congress also conveniently granted a long-delayed veteran bonus in June 1936 over FDR's veto. Although FDR vetoed the bonus making a display of frugality in the midst of his own give-away plans, the Democratic Congress was looking out for its own reelection in 1936. Both Hoover and Roosevelt had earlier denied the bonus. In Hoover's case, his denial had triggered the infamous burning of the veteran encampment (summer 1932) in Washington DC by such later illustrious soldiers as Macarthur, Eisenhower and Patton.

Earlier Roosevelt had received a "slush" fund of $48 billion in April 1935 from his rubber-stamp Congress supposedly for work relief measures. He quickly allocated $13.6 billion more than the original funds. When the Comptroller General objected to and denied the excess funds, Roosevelt was reported to have been angry (Anderson, ibid.).

So with two "display" fronts of hardball politics, FDR was said to have been extremely eager to defeat the Republican candidate Alf Landon. Of course, as the incumbent President with access to billion of dollars of taxpayers' money to fund the President's largesse, poor Landon never had a chance; he lost by over 11 million votes.

The Roosevelt Recession (1937-38) With such a popular mandate, Roosevelt went after some new villains in early 1937 – the nine "old men" of the Supreme Court. Earlier in May of 1935 the court had ruled the National Industrial Recovery Act (NRA) unconstitutional. Earlier in February 1935 the court had ruled that the elimination of gold payment clauses in government contracts was also unconstitutional. And in January 1936 the court invalidated the Agricultural Adjustment Act. FDR fumed at the court for disrupting his plans. He told the country the court's decisions were delaying the recovery. Inwardly his egoism hated any thwarting of his endeavors.

So, like any demagogue who won't admit to wrong policies, he lashed out at others, this time the court. In early 1937, he requested from Congress a bill to allow him to add six more justices to the Supreme Court, justices who would support him rather than oppose him. His reading of his victory mandate had been wrong. The country opposed this outright grasp for dictatorial control of the third checks and balances institution of the Constitution. He already had control of the executive office and the Democratic Congress. Even conservative Democrats cried out against this move as did some of the original members of the brain trust.

Business reacted adversely to the court packing. After the NRA was declared unconstitutional in May 1935, the stock market immediately rallied followed by a business rally starting in August, both of which lasted until early 1937. After the court-packing scheme was announced, also in early 1937, the market plunged 34%, rallied a bit and then plunged to a low in March 1938. Business followed the market down reaching a low in May 1938.

During the rally from May 1935 to early 1937, unemployment reached a low of 12%, the lowest since 1930 and then rose to nearly 19% in 1938. This was Roosevelt's recession 1937-38. Having a recession in the midst of a depression is an unusual event but it was Roosevelt's own fault for once again undermining the confidence of the business community with his court-packing scheme.

It also illustrates that with the removal of the hated NRA as well as the billions of tax dollars spent to win the 1936 election, the business rally created jobs. The rally stopped not only because of the court-packing idea but also because of growing labor turmoil in 1937-38 as a result of the Wagner Act that encouraged unionization and higher wages. Labor took the Act at its word especially in Detroit where attempts to unionize autoworkers resulted in bloodshed.

Roosevelt's recession finally ended in 1938 after the Democratic Congress, wary of the rising unemployment, repealed the Undistributed Profits Tax in early 1938. FDR sharply criticized the Congress for their disloyalty and even tried to purge some of the opposing Democratic Senators from the ticket in the 1938 mid-term election. Discontent with FDR and his New Deal policies showed up in the mid-term election as Republicans made some gains in Congress.

After the repeal of the distribution tax law, the stock market and business rallied a bit in the last half of 1938-39. Unemployment dropped from nearly 19% in 1938 to 16.7% in 1939. By January of 1940, it was still 14.6%, or nearly 9 million unemployed (Schlaes, ibid.).

The evidence is clear cut that whenever one of Roosevelt's socialistic laws, stripping assets from the rich, was passed, economic activity slowed and unemployment rose. Just the opposite occurred whenever one of the hated laws was found unconstitutional or repealed: economic activity rose and unemployment dropped.

One would think that Roosevelt and his advisors would have noticed the correlation and changed policies. But that was not to be. His egotistical stubbornness saw to that. It was the greedy rich not cooperating that were to blame for the slowness of the recovery; it was the out-dated gold standard restricting the economy; it was the nine "old men" of the Supreme Court holding back job creation; it was disloyal Democratic Senators undermining his endeavors. Everyone or everything was to blame except him or his policies.

An objective observer examining the 1930s unemployment rates in the Roosevelt years would have had to conclude that Roosevelt's policies and his brain trust's socialistic advice were an abject failure in creating jobs. It is very likely, given his biased adherence to penalizing the rich, that the depression would have extended well into the 1940s if World War II hadn't come along and energized the economy as well as putting millions of unemployed into the armed services.

In the 1940 Presidential election, FDR's campaign rhetoric had shifted from the greedy, rich villains to the Republican evil villains who, he said, had impeded war preparedness because of their isolationist views. Some observers credited his third-term victory to "not wanting to change horses in midstream" with war looming on the horizon. But his easy win over Wendell Wilkie by some five million votes suggests that most voters still considered him their champion regardless of his poor record in producing jobs over the past eight years. In a democracy where most voters are unsophisticated and under educated, the demagogic candidate always seems to win.

Franklin Delano Roosevelt's hold over the American voter of the 1930s was exactly the situation the Founding Fathers feared the most. When they wrote the Constitution, they created a republic not a democracy. They set up a voting requirement of owning property because they thought such a person would probably also have an education to match, thereby avoiding an unsophisticated, uneducated mass voting into office glib-tongued demagogues. When Andrew Jackson lost the election for President in 1924, his Democratic Congressional backers were instrumental in getting the property requirement to vote changed. Henceforth it was one man, one vote until 1920 when women were also allowed to vote.

Jackson's backers realized that if voting required property, Jackson wouldn't win. The average citizen didn't have property (nor education) like the citizens of the east coast original states that had always voted for a Virginia or a Massachusetts President. Their success in changing the rules to allow Jackson to win is illustrated by the number of popular votes Jackson received in the elections of 1824 and 1828 – 153,000 in 1824, 647,000 in 1828. The country ceased to be a republic in the 1828 election; henceforth it would be a democracy where all voted with no property or education requirement – just the situation the Founders feared. FDR personified their fear.

Unintended Consequences Often in the real world, a person's or a country's actions have future results that the person or country carrying out the action never considered at the time, indeed never even dreamed of in most cases. For example, the assassin who shot the Crown Prince of Austria in June 1914 probably never intended nor expected a world war in which millions were killed would be the eventual result of his actions. Similarly, unintended consequences in the 1920s and 30s brought horrifying results to America and eventually the world.

Benjamin Strong There is no doubt that the last thing Benjamin Strong intended when he started "fine tuning" the American economy in 1922 was to cause a stock market crash in 1929 that would lead to the longest, most severe depression in the 1930s that the country ever experienced. His main intent was to smooth out the ups and downs of the economic cycles so that the country would never again have to go through the financial hardships of the 1920-21 depression. After the 1929 crash, critics asserted that the Federal Reserve Board's periodical easy money and credit policies were the main cause of the crash. Board members, however, always denied any responsibility.

In any case, once the commercial rate for broker call loans rose to 10-12% while the Federal Reserve rate stood at 5%, Strong lost control of the situation. Outside money, pouring into call loans to take advantage of the attractive high rates, made his efforts at stopping market speculation superfluous. His death in October

1928, a year before the crash, mercifully shielded him from what he would have found excruciatingly painful.

Hoover and the Republicans After the October 1929 crash, not everyone expected a depression to follow let alone a severe one. In the 1907-08 and 1920-21 crashes and following depressions, although severe, were essentially over in just two years. In the first, J. P. Morgan and a pool of banks provided millions to support the system. In the second, the Federal Reserve banks provided hundreds of millions to the system by purchasing open market securities. In both cases, the quick expansive support limited the downturn's extent to two years.

In 1930, however, even though the Federal Reserve System was engaged in providing one billion dollars via security purchases to forestall a depression, the Republican-controlled Congress passed the highest tariff bill (The Hawley-Smoot Act) the country ever had in June 1930, effectively neutralizing the expansive effect of the Federal Reserve's purchasing efforts. High Republican tariffs had always been the way to preserve American jobs but it was a foolish blunder of Congress at this vulnerable time. Equally foolish was Herbert Hoover's signing of the bill over the protest of the country's economists.

What the bill did was cut off our trade with the rest of the world. This meant that the $1.5 billion on average that the US made in activity on that trade was denied to the country just at the time the country desperately needed the money to keep the economy going.

More importantly, as future results revealed, we essentially exported our pending depression all over the world, especially to Germany. It had been struggling to pay its war debts and maintain a stable economy since their defeat in WWI. The cut off of trade to the US pushed it into a severe depression. Export factories were forced to close, thousands more lost their jobs and labor clashes between communists and nationalistic labor groups occurred almost daily in the city streets.

In such turmoil, demagogues flourish and Adolph Hitler was no exception. His political party, the National Socialist Party, praying on the fears and prejudices of the people, preached anti-communist law and order, railed against the Jews and French and promised to restore German pride, as well as provide jobs and prosperity to the defeated country.

As with the Roosevelt vote, the German voters chose food on the table, a roof over their heads and a stable economy. In the three national elections, beginning in September 1930 and ending in July 1932, the National Socialists led by Hitler became the majority party in the Reichstag. The people were desperate – over five million were unemployed in 1931 – Hitler's message resonated with hope. When another moderate government collapsed, President Hindenburg turned reluctantly to Hitler to be the new Chancellor on January 30, 1933.

Hitler immediately started to provide jobs by rearming the country. His long-range plan was to revenge the humiliating defeat of Germany in the first war. Soon the factories were humming, the people had jobs and Germany regained its pride. But the people paid a terrible price for believing in Hitler. They sacrificed the Jews, devastated their population and destroyed their country. It was truly a devil's bargain.

One can only wonder what Hoover and the Republicans thought about their enabling role in Hitler's rise, his concentration camps and his bloody conquests in the years that followed the Hawley-Smoot Tariff. It is very likely they didn't see (or allow themselves to see) their connection with Hitler. It's a classic, sad case of unintended consequences.

Unfortunately the same thing happened across the world in the Pacific when Japan fell into a depression as the result of curtailed trade with the US due to the high tariff. Just as in Germany, Japan's export industry collapsed, factories closed and jobs were lost. All economic sections were soon engulfed in the depression; the moderate government fell and the ever-present militaristic party took over. They preached hatred toward the Americans for subjecting Japan to such economic hardships and starvation. They vowed revenge and enacted a policy to gain control of all necessary foreign resources by conquest. In 1931, they entered Manchuria; China became the next victim in 1937. In 1941, it was southeastern Asia to gain control of oil and rubber resources. On December 7, 1941 it was the promised revenge attack on the US at Pearl Harbor.

It boggles the mind to think that when the Republicans passed a mere tariff bill that was signed by President Hoover, it set into action a series of events that nearly destroyed the civilized world. Six million Jews were murdered, nearly 300,000 American troops were killed and countless millions of civilians lost their lives during the war not to mention the deaths of military troops of all the other countries involved. It was indeed horrendous and the worst set of unintended consequences of all time.

Roosevelt and the Democrats Amity Shlaes (ibid.) reports that in 1934, one of Roosevelt's brain trust advisors was perplexed that the depression was lingering on. One can only surmise from such perplexity that the New Dealers' original intent in imposing socialistic controls on the banking and business community was to make the depression disappear and to restore jobs to the workers. As we have seen, they failed. The unintended consequence of the socialistic controls was continued unemployment and an extended depression.

The fact that they stubbornly pursued their socialistic agenda in the face of continued economic hardship makes one wonder if the struggling people were their main concern at all. It would appear that they viewed the depression not in human terms but as a once in a lifetime opportunity to fix the "evils" of the capitalistic system. With the egotistical Roosevelt, one can't rule out the additional motive of self-aggrandizement.

Whatever the motivation, the fact remains that the New Dealers' socialistic "experiments" were at the peoples' expense. The wealthy, although relieved of assets by Roosevelt and the Democratic Congress who rubber stamped the President's request of bills, were able to survive the depression without much change in their life style. In medical experiments when the agenda procedures aren't working, the experiment is stopped to save patient's distress as well as to reexamine the procedures. Roosevelt and his New Dealers did nothing of the kind. Even as late as 1938, they were still blaming business and the wealthy for not cooperating to produce jobs. A socialist's agenda is not easily surrendered.

There was one other major unintended consequence that grew out of the depression and the socialists' attempt to fix capitalism. When FDR devalued the gold standard in 1933 and the Democratic Congress allowed him to fix the price of gold, it created a precedent for a paper money backed economy that is still with the country in the 21st Century. Some economists refer to it as fiat money issued whenever necessary by government directive. In foreign exchange, it has no fixed value as with the gold standard. Instead the exchange rate "floats" depending upon the strength and stability of the country's economy and politics. For example, if at one time the American economy and politics are extremely strong and the English economy less so, one dollar might be worth one English pound. If at another time the conditions are reversed, one English pound might be worth two dollars meaning it would now take two dollars to buy one English pound where before it took only one.

Giving up the gold standard lost two important assets. First, because of the legally fixed amount of gold backing a dollar, no increase of dollars was possible without an increase in gold supply. Hence, no inflation (or very little) is possible when on the gold standard; the value of the dollars remains essentially the same.

This means that the amount of the gold supply acts as a restriction on any expansive growth like a governor on a car restricting the speed of the car. It also means that prices and wages remain relatively stable. Alan Greenspan (ibid.) reports that on the gold standard between 1870-1913, prices rose only two-tenths percent per year or 8.6% in 43 years. That would mean that a ten-cent loaf of bread in 1870 would only cost eleven cents in 1913. Conversely between 1939 and 2006 on a fiat money standard, consumer prices rose fifteen times making a twenty five cent loaf of bread in 1939, $3.75 in 2006.

The only people who really benefit from the fiat money policy are the politicians who can issue and spend any amount of money they wish and for any purpose they want including ingratiating themselves with the voters. There is no upper limit as with the gold standard; the only limit the politicians' own conscience, honesty and scruples, which are usually oxymorons when applied to politicians.

The fiat money policy now active for 75 years has resulted in the current (2010) nearly twelve trillion dollars national debt. In contrast, while on the gold standard in 1920 after the then-costly World War I, the national debt was only $25.9 billion. In 1930, still on the gold standard, the debt had been paid down to $16.1 billion. By the end of the 1930s, after eight years of fiat money of the Roosevelt regime, the national debt had climbed to $42.9 billion. It is interesting to see how the debt climbs as well as the cost of living with the deficit spending of the Federal government in the years after 1940.

It is very probable that Roosevelt and his advisors didn't even consider the unintended consequence of devaluing the gold standard in 1933. Would they have even comprehended an $12 trillion dollar debt in just 75 years in a supposedly rich country? There is a strong possibility that the unintended consequences of compromising the gold standard in favor of a fiat money economy that encourages deficit spending will eventually have a more profound effect on the longevity of the United States than any other financial event or war in our history. Bankrupting a country in the 21st Century is much easier than many think – a national debt soaring beyond comprehension doesn't leave much wiggle room in the event of a financial emergency.

Chapter Five

World War II Expansion/1949-1950 Recession

When Roosevelt took the country off the old gold standard in 1933 and went to a paper money economy allowing unlimited Federal government spending, it set the precedent for the rest of the century for deficit spending. With it came the ever-increasing national debt and the specter of continuous inflation raising prices and wages before the onset of inevitable recessions. It's a legacy of FDR's that is not usually talked about.

Without any limit on government spending, politicians use deficit spending to their advantage. To get elected and re-elected, politicians promise tax cuts and spending on social programs. The unsophisticated voters, always voting their pocketbook, almost always elect such "generous" candidates. But tax cuts mean less government revenues and social program spending means higher government expenditure. Both add up to deficit spending at year's end, being in the red rather than in the black financially. Both also increase the money in the economy. When the money becomes greater than the available goods, an inflationary spiral begins.

With excess money chasing sparse goods, prices rise. Merchants know the consumer has excess money and is willing to pay higher prices for the limited amount of goods available. So the merchant raises prices.

At first, this stimulates the economy. With consumers and business spending the excess money, manufacturers hustle to raise production to meet the increased demand. Loans are taken out, workers are hired and more materials purchased. The rising prices, however, eventually trigger labor discontent; they want raises to keep up with the rising prices and commonly will use strikes to get them.

At the same time, the rising prices are eroding the purchasing value of the dollar. Lenders, to make up for the decreasing dollar value, increase the interest they demand on their loans. Both the wage raises and the interest increases cut into the profit of the manufacturers and businesses. Also at the same time, the rising prices create consumer resistance to further buying; unpurchased goods stay on the shelf.

As business profits fall, production slows down to meet the decreased demand; business loans decline, workers are laid off. The layoffs add to the reduction in consumer spending – demand drops even further and more workers are laid off. What at first stimulated the economy now spirals it downward into a recession. If the downward spiral is severe and deep enough, the recession will evolve into a depression.

So what started out as just another politician stratagem to get elected, in a paper money economy, such government deficit largesse almost always evolves into an inflationary spiral. The voter lured into voting for tax cuts or social program spending could easily lose his or her job several years down the line. "Several years later" is usually beyond the average voter's memory so the fiscally irresponsible politician generally escapes all blame. Indeed, if the opposing political party is in power when the recession hits, the voters' wrath is directed toward that unfortunate party and will indeed vote once again for the candidate dangling the biggest tax cut and spending program. In many cases it is the same politician whose irresponsible promises caused the inflationary spiral in which they lost their job in the first place. Such is FDR's legacy.

Which brings us to the World War II expansive policies he and the Democratic Party used to fund the war. Benjamin Anderson (ibid.) predicted in May 1945 just such an inflationary spiral as described above after World War II because of the excess money building up in the consumer's hands during the war, which commendable after the sparse, grim years of the Great Depression, nevertheless placed an enormous amount of money in the economy. Money in circulation in April 1945 was $20.1 billion. Demand deposits at commercial banks hit $91.6 billion at the end of 1944 (ibid., p. 555). War saving's bonds, which could be redeemed at any time, stood at $43.3 billion (ibid., p. 546). In contrast, money in circulation before the war in June 1939 was only $7 billion. So even before the war ended, consumers could put their hands on over $130 billion to purchase goods after the war.

This meant, as Anderson tried to warn the government but was ignored, a perfect inflationary spiral situation once the war ended (too much money, too few goods). And that's exactly what happened in 1946-47. Even before that in the last months of 1945 after Japan's surrender, labor began agitating for higher wages in anticipation of higher prices once the wartime price and wage controls were removed on June 30, 1946. A steel strike was settled in February 1946 and soon railroad worker and coal miner strikes followed.

Once the price-wage controls were lifted, the pent-up demand of consumers with money in their pockets for goods drove prices up some 33% in the next year. Even a reintroduction of modified price controls in late July of 1946 couldn't stem the tide. Food, clothing and housing prices soared and labor unrest was everywhere. A plethora of strikes crippled the nation.

President Truman had the simplistic notion that rising prices could be curtailed by extending price controls after their original termination at the end of June 1946. What he didn't seem to realize or perhaps ignored to favor the consumer/voter side of prices was that prices also determined the production of consumer goods. If it cost a manufacturer $100 (materials, wages, marketing, shipping and overhead costs) to make an item and he could only sell it legally at $110, that wasn't much of an incentive to increase production. As long as production was limited by price controls, the relationship between demand and supply could never be balanced and prices would continue to rise. Extending price controls for another year (July 1946 – July 1947) merely prolonged the inflationary spiral and postponed the inevitable recession.

The voters, sick of rising prices and the labor turmoil, voted their pocketbooks in the 1946 mid-term election and ousted the Democrats. The Republicans, for the first time in 16 years, controlled both Houses of Congress and also won three quarters of the state governorships. To make matters even worse for Truman and the Democrats, the Republicans used the opportunity to pass the labor-restrictive Taft-Hartley Act and the 22nd Constitutional amendment limiting a President to only two terms, passing it on to the Republican-controlled state legislatures to ratify. When the modified price control bill expired in July 1947, the Republicans didn't bother to extend it over Truman's objections.

Truman railed against the Republicans in his 1948 Presidential campaign for allowing prices to rise by not extending price controls. He also boasted that the Democrats had raised the total national income from less than $40 billion when they first took power in 1933 to $203 billion by 1947. He didn't seem to see the connection between that latter huge figure and the inflationary spiral that plagued his administration. All that net income chasing too few goods is the classic cause of inflation.

In their two years in power (1947-48), the Republicans couldn't stem the tide of inflation either. In the 1948 Presidential election, the fickle voters returned the Democrats to power. The rising prices continued as did labor's attempts to raise wages to mach the prices. When consumer resistance to further price rises kicked in, production fell. The decrease was reinforced by the higher wage and materials cost manufacturers had to pay as well as by the higher interest rates on business loans that lenders demanded to make up for the devalued dollar.

The inflation spiral recession finally hit in 1949-50 when thousands lost their jobs further adding to declining demand and production. It had taken four years after the war for the inflationary cycle to run its course culminating in the inevitable recession. By that time, few probably realized that the entire cycle had been caused years before during the war by Roosevelt's expansive easy money policy to fund the war. Once the easy money was in the consumers' pocket and supply of consumers' goods strictly limited, the entire cycle was inevitable.

To climb out of the inevitable recession back to balance requires either patience or, in the modern world, a cautious stimulation. With the 1949-50 recession, it was the Korean War of 1950 and its required war goods spending that supplied the stimulation.

Chapter Six

Eisenhower Years 1953-1961

The eight years (1953-1961) that the Republican Dwight Eisenhower occupied the Presidency are unique in the country's political and economic history since World War II in that there were only moderate efforts to stimulate the economy. He won the 1952 election in part by promising to end the Korean War and to balance the budget. He did end the war by accepting a truce and he did manage three years (1956, 57 and 60) of budget surpluses of about $1.5 billion each year. One of the years (1959), when the deficit reached $12.4 billion, he apologized to the people.

The Eisenhower years are also unique in that, without large stimulation policies, they show just how sensitive economic ups and downs in a paper money economy are to even minor changes in the money supply. When Eisenhower ended the Korean War, government war expenditures stopped in 1953 and a one-year moderate recession followed. Government tax cuts then stimulated economic activity in 1955. The expenditures on the interstate highway system extended the activity into 1956. Even these rather moderate easy money acts had their negative effects in 1957-58 when the stimulatory effects wore off and the country entered two years of recession in which some 5.3 million workers lost their jobs.

To stimulate the economy and create jobs, Eisenhower and the Republicans were forced to pass a road construction bill in the spring of 1958 that pumped $5.5 billion into the economy over the next two years. Even though the country was coming out of the recession by the time of the 1958 mid-term elections, the voters saw only lost jobs, labor unrest and school segregation problems in the south. So they voted their pocketbooks and gave the Democrats solid control of Congress for the first time in two decades.

Eisenhower's last two years were a running battle with the Democrats trying to spend on social programs and unemployment. He used his veto and the threat of a veto to hold down spending. Nonetheless the recession period saw 40% higher spending and 60% less government revenue resulting in a deficit of $12.4 billion in 1959. The excess spending did produce a rise in economic activity in 1959 but a one-year recession in 1960 followed. As we have seen throughout the economic history of the country, every expansion period, no matter how limited, has been followed by a contraction period. What goes up must come down.

So even though the Republicans (in the 1950s) tried to hold spending down, their tax cut, interstate highway and road maintenance bills all stimulated the economy for a time only to be followed by a mild to moderate recession. Even Roosevelt in the Great Depression years, using deficit spending to stimulate the economy before the 1936 Presidential election, caused a follow-up severe recession in 1937-38. Without gold acting as a stabilizer on the economy, paper money economics are especially susceptible to ups and downs. Politicians, since the Great Depression, generate the ups but take no responsibility for the downs.

Chapter Seven

Kennedy/Johnson Expansion 1961-1969
1970s Recessions

During the 1960 Presidential election, Eisenhower was depicted by liberal commentators as a "do nothing President," soft on Communism and uncaring about the common people. They disparaged the annual 2-3% average economic growth rate during the 1950s as anemic. They advocated for a much more robust growth rate using deficit spending as pioneered by FDR.

John F. Kennedy, the Democratic candidate, picked up on this theme declaring he would get the country moving again and stand up to the Communists around the world. A minor recession in 1960 probably helped Kennedy win the election. Initially unsure about deficit spending, the struggling economy brought him around to use it. Significantly, JFK's deficit spending wasn't just to get the country out of a depression or severe recession as Keynes had advocated but rather as a policy to maintain economic growth indefinitely. In just a few years of Kennedy's economic "magic," the growth rate hit 5% and unemployment fell. To liberal economists, this was the pathway to a prosperous future. Soon it became the accepted policy, even for the Republicans, for the rest of the century and beyond. Deficit spending had arrived.

Kennedy's programs included a major tax cut, minimum wage raise, increase of Social Security benefits, housing and health aid, job training, a going-to-the-moon program and others. All of which poured Federal money into the economy. Kennedy introduced 165 bills and a compliant Democratic Congress passed 108 of them (Lorant, 1968).

After Kennedy was assassinated in November 1963, Lyndon B. Johnson, the Vice President, succeeded him. According to his biographers, LBJ was egotistical and arrogant and wanted to be rated as a great President right up there with Washington, Lincoln and the Roosevelts. Like Andrew Jackson, he was a backcountry Populist with the common touch that would do anything to display his innate sense of superiority by including giving away the key to the Treasury. Not only did he get Kennedy's $10 billion tax cut passed, he did JFK one better by enacting a Great Society program that included Medicare, a war on poverty, aid to education, and a Civil Rights bill.

All these programs and bills poured billions into the economy and would continue to do so indefinitely. For example, in order to get the Medicare program passed, he had to promise the American Medical Association (who considered the program socialized medicine and threatened to lobby against it) not to cap doctor fees but to allow "reasonable" raises in the future. This was a gross mistake on his part. His aides had projected a $10 billion total cost in ten years for Medicare. Instead with the "reasonable" clause, the cost for Medicare in doctor's fees alone reached $70 billion in ten years (and is still climbing).

Starting in 1961, the billions poured into the economy pushed economic activity upwards at a staggering rate reaching in 1967 more than twice the rate displayed during the Roaring Twenties. Only the brief World War II rate outdid the Sizzling Sixties.

Johnson should have been jubilant by the adulation he received for his Great Society program but no sooner had he signed the Civil Right's Bill in the summer of 1964, then he was angered by the "ingratitude of the blacks" (he called them the "n" word) who rioted in Detroit. Some 150 riots and city burnings erupted throughout the rest of the decade.

During the Presidential campaign in 1964, angered by the Republican's charge that he was soft on Communism, he used the Tonkin Gulf incident off of South Vietnam to increase the American military presence in the war between South Vietnam and Communist North Vietnam. Up to that point, it had been a civil war with American military advisors working with the South. The incident involved a North Vietnamese patrol boat apparently firing on an American destroyer in the middle of the night. According to biographers, Johnson knew it was a false report but immediately ordered the bombing of North Vietnamese ports and sent thousands of US troops to South Vietnam.

Based on the timing of his actions just before the election, biographers have inferred that he used the incident to quiet his distracters thereby insuring that he would win the election. One has to wonder if he even thought about the lives of American troops that would be lost because of his egotistical need to win an election and show his peers that he was indeed number one. Eventually some 55,000 American lives would be lost because of his decision. It has been said of Johnson that behind an amiable façade lay a cynical manipulator of power.

As it turned out, the Tonkin Gulf incident initiated his fall from grace. Not only did he eventually end up sending close to 250,000 troops but also the war expenditures surged to the point where, combined with all the billions poured into the economy from the tax cut and Great Society programs, prices started to rise higher, wage demands surfaced and severe inflation infiltrated the economy. By 1967, rising interest rates undermined production and an economic downturn spread across the country. Consumer price resistance appeared along with layoffs as the economy sagged into a minor recession. The 10% surcharge on income tax that Johnson needed to pay for his war was the last straw. By the time of the 1968 Presidential election, the economy had hit bottom. Johnson, seeing his popularity ratings falling, increasing student turmoil against the war and the country stuck in a recession, decided not to seek re-election. There is nothing worse to an egotist than to lose.

Even still, with voters voting their pocketbooks and a yearning for peace and law and order, Richard Nixon, the Republican candidate, didn't win by much. His promise to end the war probably gave him the winning margin.

The 1970s Inflation/Recessions After Nixon was elected in 1968, he benefited by a one-year economic recovery in 1969. By 1970, however, the country entered a two-year recession. Five million workers would eventually lose their jobs. The inflationary spiral initiated by the Kennedy-Johnson spending and reinforced by the Vietnam War costs was fueled by over $61.2 billion in deficit spending between 1960 and 1968. Nixon's administration, partly because of layoffs and less consumer demand as well as less tax revenue, posted another $42.6 billion to the national debt in just two years. That meant that entering the 1970s, the country's money supply from 1960 to 1970 had increased by some $100 billion. It also meant a 6.2% inflation rate by the end of the 1960s.

Once the inflationary spiral starts, getting $100 billion out of the system isn't easy. It lingers, causing ever-rising prices, higher wage demands, higher production costs, higher interest rates, lower production and further layoffs, reinforcing the whole cycle. Nixon tried wage and price controls for two years, which only postponed the next recession to 1974-75 and made prices worse when they were removed. President Gerald Ford, Nixon's successor after Nixon resigned in 1974 (because of the Watergate break-in cover up) signed a $16 billion income tax rebate to stimulate a rapid recovery in mid 1975, the highest since 1950. By the first part of 1976, the economy was growing by some 9% but then slowed in the summer to 2%. Still, inflation lingered, prices still rose. The voter thought the Democrat Jimmy Carter would give them a better financial deal and voted him in as President in 1976. But Carter had no luck either in stemming the inflation – prices, wages and interest rates still rose undermining production that led to more jobs lost. By June 1978, inflation hit 9%. In 1979, it peaked at nearly 14%. The purchasing power of the dollar was eroding as never before. In October of 1979, the US Treasury ten-year note interest rate stood at 11% and commercial loan rates even higher. The higher the interest rates, the more business suffered with more bankruptcies and more failures.

Theorists believed then that as inflation rises, the rise in unemployment would curb consumer income and hence demand, gradually bringing down prices and effectively ending the inflation spiral. But throughout the 1970s, as inflation rose, so did unemployment but demand remained the same. A new word was coined, "stagflation," in which it seemed that inflation and unemployment would rise together without any decrease in demand.

It is no wonder this happened when one looks at the government expenditures for the 1970s. Not only was it enacting tax rebates, it was still paying for the Vietnam War (before it ended in 1975) and for the ever-increasing costs of Johnson's Great Society programs such as Medicare. Also, Nixon signed an annual cost-of-living adjustment (COLA) indexed to inflation for Social Security recipients and the Fed added to the money supply by open market security purchases. One can see that billions of Federal funds were still being poured into the economy even as the government was purportedly fighting inflation. The national debt for the period 1970-1980 ($541 billion) gives a rough approximation of just how much money there was in the economy driving up prices. To put this staggering amount of increased national debt into perspective, the Kennedy/Johnson/Nixon combined debt for the 1960s was $103.8 billion while Eisenhower's debt just 20 years earlier was only $27.2 billion.

And the government's national debt brought about by deficit spending wasn't the only factor in fueling inflation during the 1970s. The wide spread use of the credit card brought easy credit to millions adding to the buying power of the public and the upward pressure on prices. It is probably fair to say that upwards of $600 billion (more than one half a trillion!) was fueling the inflationary spiral of the 1970s. So, while Kennedy and Johnson's easy money and credit policies of the 1960s initiated the inflationary spiral beginning in the late 1960s, Johnson's ongoing expenditures demanded of his Great Society programs and Nixon's COLA Act reinforced and prolonged the inflation and recessions that plagued the country for the next 12 years.

Hence the title of this sector: "The 1970s Inflation/ Recessions." In many ways the "Sizzling Sixties" and the "Roaring Twenties" are similar periods in America's economic history. Both were Federal government-generated monetary expansion periods and both were followed by the inevitable results of expansion periods, i.e., the 1930s Great Depression and the 1970s inflation/recessions respectively.

Inflation and its negative effects thwarted Jimmy Carter's efforts at getting passed his promised social programs. To get re-elected in 1980, he knew he would have to curtail inflation somehow. Nothing had worked to date and it was only getting worse. He appointed Paul Volcker as the new Federal Reserve Chairman in July 1979 with the mandate to end inflation.

Volcker was a tough, take-charge guy who knew that the only way to stop inflation was to wring all the excess money and credit out of the economy. He also knew that it would be painful for the country. An instant major recession would result with more unemployment, frozen credit, business failures, home foreclosures and a very dispirited populace. Nevertheless, it had to be done and the quickest way to tighten the money supply was to raise the Federal Reserve interest rate to never before seen highs. By April 1980 the rate stood at 20%. Instant contraction of the economy was the result. No business could afford to borrow at 20%. Unemployment shot up to 11% of the labor force by late 1982. A very severe and deep recession rocked the country for the next two years. The best deal in town was the purchase of Treasury notes or bonds if one had the money to take advantage of the extremely high interest rates. This must have pleased Volcker. The purchases effectively removed money from the economy, which tightened the money supply even more.

It took two and a half years to bring down inflation to an "acceptable" level. But in a paper money economy, as long as government spends more each year than its incoming revenue, some degree of inflation will always be present. From 1988 to 2000, inflation averaged each year from 3 to 4%, going as high as 6% in 1990 to a low of 1½% in 1998.

Needless to say at this point, the inflation, high prices, unemployment and recession did in Jimmy Carter during the 1980 Presidential election. He lost to the Republican Ronald Reagan. As always, American Federal elections are about the economy, about the voter's pocketbook.

According to Robert Samuelson (*The Great Inflation and its Aftermath,* 2008, Random House, N.Y.), Reagan's firm commitment to combating inflation was just what the country needed. Reagan backed Volcker's extremely unpopular, severe tightening of the money and credit supply. Through the severe recession of his first two years and all the mean and hateful criticism from all sides, Regan stuck to his convictions. At the end of 1981, the inflation rate stood at nearly 9%; by the end of 1982, it was less than 4%. Volcker and Reagan had been correct to pursue their course. Samuelson called it a profound achievement.

Chapter Eight

Reagan Expansion 1981-1989
1989-1992 Recession

In 1980, Ronald Reagan took advantage of the country's economic woes that were saddled on Jimmy Carter by promising the voters a tax cut in his campaign speeches. Although a politically practical thing to do – nobody wins the Presidency by promising a tax raise – it was fiscally irresponsible. The national debt in 1980 stood at $930.2 billion with little chance of paying it down without a tax raise. The last big tax cut proposed by Kennedy and passed by Johnson ($11.5 billion) ended up dragging the nation through some twelve years of inflation, decreased production, unemployment and four recessions. Reagan's tax cut of $750 billion in 1981 phased out over five years was sure to have the same negative effects down the line as seen in previous expansive periods.

The tax cut did what it was supposed to do: stimulate the economy and make Reagan and the Republicans look good. No one seemed to mind that tax revenue would eventually be $750 billion less adding to the national debt that was already nearly one trillion dollars at the start of the decade. The country was happy. Consumer purchasing increased, lending soared, business prospered and unemployment fell. Of course, all that extra money in the economy also fueled inflation. By 1987, it was 3.6% and rising.

Another thing happened during those first few years of increased prosperity and which unfortunately always happens in boom times – a sense of exaggerated optimism, almost an exuberance, came over executives in the financial industry. In less prosperous times the banks and other financial companies are more cautious in their lending. In the good times, caution is thrown to the wind; formerly risky loans are now seen as big money makers. The big US banks now began lending huge sums to South American countries also suddenly booming. In short, the banks overextended themselves just as they have always done when the times are good and don't seem to have an end in sight.

Other financial companies such as the savings and loan industry also smelled profits in the winds of good times. In the 1970s, they had taken a beating as increasing inflation eroded profits from their long-term loans (usually 30 year, low interest mortgages). When the government agreed to their charters originally they were only allowed to lend on home mortgages. Now, with good times and other financial companies flourishing, they lobbied Congress to allow them to lend on any construction projects at rates keeping up with inflation.

As soon as a compliant Congress lifted the restrictions, newly minted "developers" crawled out of the woodwork and got S&L loans. Soon the country was awash in tacky, little roadside shopping malls, small business complexes, unnecessary resorts and hotels. When the saturation point arrived and mall shops couldn't be rented nor resort or hotel rooms filled, the loans went into default. At the same time, arrogant, unscrupulous S&L executives were living high on the hog with depositors' money buying company jets for personal use, going on resort junkets charging them to the company, and lending company deposits to close friends for projects later to be worthless. It wasn't long before many S&Ls were insolvent requiring the Federal government to reimburse their depositors and take over operations. The total cost to the government was said to have ranged between $90 to $120 billion which was added to the national debt to avoid a credit freeze.

The big banks were equally inept in the 1980s. When their risky loans made to Latin America went into default in the mid 1980s, they took huge losses. Recklessly trying to recoup, they started lending at a stepped-up pace to domestic commercial real estate developers creating a boom in such real estate as skyscrapers, condos, huge enclosed shopping malls and large housing projects. Here too, just as with the S&Ls, overbuilding soon undermined profits and the loans went into default. The real estate boom collapsed, the banks took huge losses and entrenched, stopped lending and created a credit collapse throwing the country into a recession in the fall of 1989.

Again the government had to face the possibility that the bank collapse and credit crunch could lead to a very severe recession or even a depression. So between July 1989 to July 1992, the Federal Reserve Board was forced to begin a 23-step process of gradually lowering its fund rate to spark the economy. Recovery was slow.

Inflation reached 6.25% at the end of 1990 while unemployment was over 7% in the middle of 1992. Millions were out of work.

Adding to the economic turmoil of the late 1980s and early 90s was the volatile actions of the stock market. Reagan's tax cut stimulation of the early 80s also produced a rising stock market and an increasing number of corporate mergers and takeovers. One of the most profitable means to make money in boom times is for ambitious financial players to acquire corporations by merger, buy out or takeover with borrowed funds. Once acquired, thousands of workers are cut to lower costs and make the companies, or portions of them, more attractive for sale. Once sold, the loans are paid off and the "entrepreneur" who had the chutzpah to make the acquisition pockets a handsome profit.

Republican leaders and conservative economists seem to think this acquisition process represents the epitome of laissez-faire capitalism. Out with the old, inefficient corporation, in with the new efficient one. Other, more liberal thinkers see the process as parasitic on the system. Nothing is produced for the market, only profit for the risk takers. The laid off workers surely don't profit – lives are interrupted, plans are destroyed, financial stabilizers lost. Somehow their tales get pushed under the carpet. It seems that Republican administrations, enamored of capitalism, rubber stamp approval of these capitalized acquisitions more readily than Democrats. "Competition" is the main approval parameter rather than unemployment.

Reagan's stimulation of the economy actually lasted about five years. The 1986 savings and loan debacle plus the huge losses the big banks took on their Latin American loans and later their real estate loans may have been the first signs of trouble ahead. The stock market, however, kept on rising, as it and the country didn't seem to notice the upward "creep" of inflation and prices. What finally made the market take a second look was the Federal Reserve Board under its new chairman Alan Greenspan raising its fund rate on September 4, 1987 from 5.5 to 6%. That, combined with the Federal government in October blocking tax deductions for debt incurred in corporate takeovers seems to have precipitated the historic October 19, 1987 stock market crash of 508 points. At that time, it was the second largest one-day drop ever at 23%. Only the 24% one-day drop on December 12, 1914 during the anxiety of World War I was greater.

Fearing another 1929 and the dire after effects, the Federal Reserve Open Market Committee (FOMC) approved the purchase of billions of Treasury securities right after the crash to support the financial system and the economy. This also added to the growing national debt during the Reagan expansion years.

The fact that the financial system was being supported by the FOMC's buying of securities fueled a rapid recovery of the economy in late 1987 and early 1988. By March, the FOMC started selling securities to take money out of the system and slow economic activity. It also raised its fund rate back to 6.5% to tighten the money supply and combat rising inflation. About this time, the real estate boom, fueled by big bank loans for a number of years, finally collapsed. As mentioned earlier, the big banks (after taking two big hits – the earlier Latin American loan defaults and now the real estate loan defaults) retreated from the active scene, hunkered down, drew in their loans, and stopped lending new ones. A credit freeze ensued and the 1989-92 recession began in the fall of 1989. The banks came begging to the government to be bailed out (more additions to the national debt) and the Federal Reserve Board began its three year reduction of the federal funds rate incorporating 23 reductions in all trying to breathe life back into the economy. As mentioned though, millions (or 7% of the labor force) lost their jobs by 1992.

Poor George Bush, Reagan's Republican successor in 1988, won the Presidency before the economic sky had started to fall. Reagan's expansion policy of tax cut stimulation that led inevitably to contraction and a recession, all fell on Bush's head. In the country's mind, the man in the White House at the time of an economic collapse is to blame, pure and simple. In an electorate totally economically ignorant, nothing else would be expected.

To make the recession worse, in 1990 Bush raised the income tax breaking his 1988 campaign promise to the voters of "no new taxes." It was an attempt to reduce the fast-growing yearly deficit that was beginning to worry everyone. It was eerily reminiscent of Herbert Hoover raising the income tax in 1932 supposedly as a sign to business that the government was doing its part in the depression to balance the budget so they should do theirs by increasing production and employment.

In the election of 1992, even though the 23 Reserve reductions in the funds rate were finally having an effect in turning around the economy, George Bush lost to William Clinton running on "it's the economy stupid!" slogan (it always is!). Clinton only received 43% of the vote to Bush's 37%. The third candidate, Independent Ross Perot, playing on some people's fears over the constant deficits and the then-staggering national debt of $3.2 trillion (1990), received 19% of the vote probably denying Bush the votes he needed to win.

So there we have it. Another politician's irresponsible stimulation package to get elected, ending in financial turmoil, unemployment and personal grief years later. Politicians and voters should ask themselves what they got for all the money spent during the Reagan expansion program and Bush's involuntary contraction end result. When Reagan entered office in 1981, the national debt was around $980 billion, nearly one trillion dollars. At the end of his two terms in 1988, the debt stood at $2.68 trillion. In the middle of Bush's term (1990), the debt reached $3.2 trillion, and at the end of his term (1992) the debt was $4.1 trillion. Overall, between Reagan and Bush the national debt increased from nearly one trillion to over four trillion dollars in just twelve years.

For all that money, did we have a stable economy? Did we have full employment with jobs at a decent wage? Did we avoid inflation and rising prices? Did we have responsible lending practices? Did we avoid a stock market crash? Did our medical bills stabilize? The answer to all of these questions is, of course, "No." Indeed, just the opposite happened for each question. We didn't have a stable economy nor did we avoid inflation and rising prices nor did banks and S&Ls exercise responsible lending practices, etc.

To be fair, Reagan's huge spending on defense did play a major part in the dissolution of the Soviet Union in 1989 and in the winning of the Gulf War in 1990. While Johnson's on-going Medicare, Great Society programs and other Congressional social spending programs added greatly to the total debt.

But the unbudgeted bank and S&L bailouts as well as the billions in unemployment compensation for workers who lost their jobs because of mergers, buyouts, takeovers and the recession can be directly attributed to Reagan's stimulation-inflation-recession cycle. With all the debt and negative effects, one has to question whether the policy of deficit spending is really a rational means to provide a stable economy. It seems that the only people who profit from it are the politicians using it to get elected and re-elected as well as bank and corporate executives who irresponsibly take advantage of the government largesse. The little guys (the workers) end up taking the brunt of the financial debacles and collapses.

Chapter Nine

Clinton Years 1993-2001/2000-2002 Recession

Like his predecessors Kennedy and Reagan, William Clinton ingratiated himself with the voters by promising a large tax cut and job training programs in his 1992 Presidential campaign. They were sold to the voters as a means to getting out of the 1989-1992 recession. With the national debt at $4.1 trillion, the annual deficits running around $150 billion and the unemployment rate above 7%, it was a fiscally irresponsible promise. Pouring money into the economy might have a short-term stimulus but it would also have a long-term effect in raising inflation and more unemployment.

Confronted with fiscal reality after being elected, Clinton listened to his economic advisors to forego the easy-money policies in favor of fiscal discipline in reducing the annual deficits. Business and the public liked the new discipline especially after having suffered through a 6% inflation rate only a few years before. The economy rebounded growing over 5% the rest of 1993. Inflation dropped below 3% and unemployment started inching down. Alan Greenspan feared the growth was too robust and started raising the Federal fund interest rate from 3.2% in February 1994 to 5.5% by the end of the year. The end result was the famous "soft landing" of the economy in 1995. Greenspan was praised for his "adept" handling of the economy accomplished with adequate growth, increased jobs, and inflation below 3%.

Indeed, although Clinton was the President through most of the 1990s, it was Alan Greenspan as Chairman of the Federal Reserve Board who dominated economic policy. One board member who resigned after only two years complained that Greenspan made all the fund-rate decisions after only perfunctory discussions with the other members. Other critics also disputed Greenspan's popular "maestro" image for positive policies. For instance, some critics believed that Greenspan, in response to what he perceived as too robust growth and inflation fears after the Fed's easing of the money and credit supply immediately following the 1987 market crash, raised the Federal fund interest rate too fast in 1988. This resulted, they say, in a tightened money and credit market forcing the banks into a credit crunch situation bringing about the 1989-1992 recession.

When Greenspan accomplished his "soft landing" of the economy at the end of 1995, he had raised the fund rate to 5.5%. That year also saw the beginning of the dot.com stock boom. The first Initial Public Offering (IPO) for a dot.com company with no profit on its books took place in August. The stock market loved it. The stock opened at $28 and closed the first day at $71. The insiders made a fortune and soon every other profitless dot.com company had IPOs wanting to get some of that easy money. Company CEOs were instant millionaires as were secretaries and even warehouse workers who had accepted stock options in lieu of salary in the start-up companies. The market soared. At the start of 1995, the Dow Jones average stood at 4000; at the end of 1996 it was 6000. By the end of 1997, it was 8000 – doubled in just three years.

The economy also took off after the "soft landing." By spring of 1996, it was growing at a 6% rate. Some economists worried that the growth was too fast and too soon. The surging stock market also gave them fits. Almost every day, it hit a new historical high. It was all very remindful of the Roaring Twenties and the surging market with its awful crash of 1929. Even Greenspan showed concern with his "irrational exuberance" speech of December 5, 1996. But it was a half-hearted attempt to quell the stock market frenzy and the market sensed it, dropping only 150 points the next day before resuming its fearful climb the following day.

Greenspan was well aware of the 1920s history and the similarity of the 1990s. The problem was: When does one raise rates to curb economic growth and market exuberance and when does one lower them to stimulate? It was a fine balancing act. In 1920, the Federal Reserve Board had raised their discount rate almost overnight to 7% throwing the country into the 1920-21 depression. In the following decade, the easy money credit policy of the Fed enabled speculators to pour money into the stock market resulting in the eventual crash and the severe Great Depression that followed.

Greenspan hadn't raised the fund rate since the end of 1995. When he had lowered it at the start of the next year from 6% by a half point, the economy started growing and the market gained. By not doing anything else during 1996, the market took it as a positive sign and surged 1000 points. Perhaps to test the waters, he finally decided two months after his "irrational exuberance" speech in December 1996 to raise the rate a timid quarter point. The market promptly lost 500 points. It was at this point that his critics thought he should have continued raising the rate to slowly deflate the growing dot.com bubble thereby avoiding the 2000 crash. But Greenspan backed off, perhaps fearing that further raises would trigger a recession, something no one wanted on their record.

His "irrational exuberance" remark was a form of moral persuasion, appealing to the stock market investors' common sense to slow down their purchases. Interestingly, the 1920s Reserve Board used the same technique in trying to convince banks not to lend money to stock speculators. It, too, was a rationalized alternative to actually raising Fed rates and causing a market crash with a following recession. Just like Greenspan's attempt, it failed to curb the market.

In the 1920s, the Board dithered and debated endlessly about whether to raise rates and risk a crash or do nothing and let events play out. There has always been one faction of the Board members (especially in the 1920s) who believed that the Federal Reserve System's original mandate to stabilize he economy and accommodate business meant just that; the stock market wasn't in their jurisdiction. The other faction argued that it was, and deadlock was the result. The inaction allowed the market to keep on rushing upward to its inevitable fate.

The same scenario appears to have played out within the Board meetings once the stock market started surging in 1995. Some Board members thought a preemptive raise of the rates was the right choice; others weren't sure. Greenspan kept his own council – the statistics. Even though the market hit another historical high of 8000 by the end of 1997, unemployment had fallen to less than 5% and inflation was just below 2%, the lowest level in decades. In addition, the annual deficit was down to $22 billion. In he next three years, the deficit turned into a surplus reaching $237 billion by the year 2000. The country hadn't seen a surplus since 1969. All in all, as Greenspan surveyed the statistics, he appears to have been quite proud of the positive effects happening on his watch.

He also knew that the surging market with its high prices was inducing millions of stock options to be executed thereby increasing capital gains tax revenue to the point where budgetary surpluses became a reality. With visions of continuous surpluses helping to pay off part of the national debt, Greenspan appears to have decided that the stock market was outside his bailiwick. If the irrationally exuberant stock investors were so stupid as to keep throwing money at a market bubble that sooner or later, by all historical references would explode, then that was their problem. When the inevitable crash and recession occurred, he and the Board would then clean up the "mess."

So, Alan Greenspan did nothing to impede the stock market climb after the last rate raise in February of 1997. The market hit 9000 in mid 1998. He was forced to actually lower the Fed fund rate in the fall of 1998 after the market lost 1000 points in response to the collapsing economies in southeast Asia and Russia's default on its loans. Fearing a worldwide recession, he felt lowering the rate would provide easier credit to the world. The US stock market apparently received most of the credit. The market zoomed upward from 8000 to 10,000 (Dow Jones average) in just the first half of 1999. Before the end of the year, it had reached 11,000. The budget surplus rose from $70 billion the previous year to $124 billion for 1999. Ten-year "wishful thinking" budget projections had the surplus anywhere from $600 billion to $3 trillion total.

With surplus figures floating around like that, Congress smelled political advantage. The Democrats wanted more social program spending to ingratiate themselves with the poor and minority voters; the Republicans wanted tax cuts, also to ingratiate themselves with the full range of voters. Greenspan's hopes for paying off part of the national debt disappeared with the political parties jockeying for position. President Clinton was forced to play diplomat and give the surplus as a compromise to the Social Security fund.

The surplus occurrence is one of the best illustrations of the fiscal irresponsibility of Congress. Both parties were more concerned with re-election politics than the fiscal strength of the country. With the national debt standing at $5.6 trillion in 2000, there was no financial cushion in place to cope with any future financial calamity. Any good government, like any good bank, always has financial reserves in place to deal with financial reverses. In the surplus euphoria, however, very few people were thinking of a future calamity. Indeed, during the Clinton surplus years, any semblance of fiscal restraint by Congress disappeared into thin air. Spending caps were voided and an additional one trillion dollars of social spending over the next ten years was legislated. And, of course, earmark "pork" increased to record highs. Congressional members were like kids in a candy store. Let the good times roll!

It is amazing in retrospect to realize how ignorant our leaders are, how they can fool themselves into believing that "this time is different," that the good times will last, that surpluses are made to be spent, not to be put away for a rainy day. Unfortunately for the country, the rainy day was just over the horizon.

When the stock market zoomed upwards from 8000 to 11,000 in just the first half of 1999, the economy tagged along reaching 4.5% GDP growth in the same time period. That was extremely fast, giving even Greenspan pause. The inflation figures were also disconcerting, starting back up to 3%. His economic colleagues thought the market should be brought down 10-20% to cool off the economy.

So, on June 30, 1999, Greenspan (apparently reluctantly) raised the fund rate a quarter point without much effect on the market, which, after several years of Fed inaction, had a mind of its own. In the next seven months, however, the rate was raised from 5 to 6.5%. It had an effect. By spring 2000, the NASDAQ market had plunged 30%; it was off 50% by the end of the year. The bottom fell out of the mostly still profitless dot.com stocks, dropping 80-90%. From nearly 12,000 in March 2000, the Dow Jones average eventually plummeted to below 8000 a year later.

All the economic miseries of the 2000-02 recession staggered the country. Production dropped off, corporate profits sagged, unemployment rose into the millions, consumer demand fell, inventories rose…all the same results we've seen in the contraction period of any expansive "good times" era. In addition, the usual credit crunch as banks "hunkered down" to preserve their reserves exposed the crooked and weak companies. Enron was exposed as cooking the books to give Wall Street the impression that it was a constantly growing, highly profitable company so that the executives' stock options could be exercised at a fraudulently high stock price. World Com was exposed as being dangerously overextended with outrageous executive excesses and collapsed. None of this made the public confident in the economic future.

Further, the atrocity on September 11, 2001 deepened the recession and stunned the nation, freezing the economy until 2003.

So, the 1990s ended with a severe recession just as they had started and both had the fingerprints of Mr. Greenspan closely entangled with the beginnings of each recession. Indeed, the 1990s are a clear example of just how difficult it is to maintain a stable economy based on fiat money. For example, when Greenspan was appointed chairman of the Fed in June 1987, he inherited the inevitable inflation and contractive downturns of Reagan's five years of expansion in the 1980s. Being an obsessive inflation fighter, he quickly raised the Federal fund rate in early September 1987. He spent the next few years compensating for that fateful decision, subjecting the country to a roller coaster of first rate decreases and then increases leading to the 1989-92 recession which cost George Bush his re-election.

His next manipulation of the fund rate was to get the country out of the recession. Apparently learning about the dangers of overacting too quickly, he proceeded to gradually lower the rate, easing money and credit. The slow approach in 23 rate decreases over two years finally started to kick in just as Clinton was taking office. George Bush got the blame for the recession but Clinton got the credit for renewed growth.

Even the slow approach, though, couldn't stop rapid growth the next year so Greenspan again began raising rates to stabilize the ship. Slowly, he nudged down the economy into the famous "soft landing" in 1995 and was praised heartily for it!

His most severe test was yet to come when, in 1995, the dot.com stock craze ignited the stock market to surge the next several years to historical heights. For the most part during the years when the dot.com bubble was developing, he did nothing fearing, perhaps, that raising rates would trigger another recession even though by 1996, many economists and even Reserve Board members were calling for a "pre-emptive" raise in rates to defuse the stock market before it got out of hand. Apparently he rationalized that the surging market was good for the country, increasing the growth rate, decreasing unemployment and inflation and creating the first budget surpluses in some thirty years.

He finally raised rates in 1999 and that appears to have triggered the market crash and the 2000-02 recession immediately followed.

So, the scorecard for Chairman Greenspan in his first 13 years in office (1987-2000) was two recessions and one “soft landing.” As we shall see, his record in the new century wasn’t too impressive either.

Chapter Ten

Bush Expansion 2001-2009/2008 Great Recession

As the country entered a new decade (as well as a new century), it found itself once again mired in a recession. Indeed, it is amazing as well as dispiriting to note that ever since the creation of the Federal Reserve System in 1913, the country has entered each decade of the 20th Century mired in a recession or depression.

In 1920, it was the 1920-21 depression largely attributed to the Federal Reserve abruptly raising its discount rate. In 1930, the country entered the Great Depression, again largely attributed to the Federal Reserve Board's easy money and credit policy during the 1920s fueling the stock market's crash and the Republicans' inept handling of the economy after the crash. By 1940, the country was still in the grip of the Great Depression because of Franklin Roosevelt's refusal to include the upper-class job producers in his recovery plans. Nineteen fifty found the country still dealing with the remnants of the 1948-49 recession, the result of the World War II expansive financial policies and inflation that followed.

It was no different in 1960; the country was in another recession although a mild one. The Kennedy/Johnson expansion of the 1960s brought its first recession in 1970 on Nixon's watch and its last recession in 1979-82 engineered by the Fed Chairman Paul Volcker. To combat the rampant high inflation, he had to raise the Fed interest rate to historic levels which triggered the recession. And we have just discussed the 1989-92 recession opening the 1990s and the dot.com bubble recession starting in the 2000 market crash. And now another in 2010.

It is a very discouraging record when one considers that the Federal Reserve System was created to eliminate these economic downturns and provide economic stability for the country. Instead, it seems that the Fed and politicians have produced more recessions or depressions than avoiding them.

Not only was it more of the same economic miseries when 2000 arrived but it was also more of the same fiscally irresponsible Presidential candidates promising massive expansive tax cuts to ingratiate themselves with voters and to "get the country moving again."

George Bush II, the Republican, promised a $1.6 trillion tax cut, Al Gore, the Democrat, $700 billion. With the country entering a recession during the 2000 election and a stock market collapse then currently happening, all while the Democrat Clinton was in office, one would expect the American voter to once again oust the old party and vote their pocketbooks opting at the same time for the larger tax cut. A Republican-controlled Congress, however, made the choice difficult. Who was to blame for the financial fiasco? The Democratic President and his economic advisors or the Republican Congress? A conservative Supreme Court had to finally choose: Bush over Gore.

No one seemed to be concerned at the time that either promised tax cut would add appreciably to the national debt that stood at $5.6 trillion when Bush took office. No one seemed to care that the debt had gone up $1.5 trillion during Clinton's years in office even though his administration supposedly practiced fiscal restraint with four years of budget surplus of over $500 billion. If a fiscal restraint policy and budget surpluses during a time of robust prosperity couldn't make a dent in the national debt, when would the debt ever be repaid? As events turned out in the next decade, it would appear that America would never be able to pay down its debt. It would constantly rise until the value of the dollar would fall to a low point where no foreign country would buy our debt and America would have to declare bankruptcy. Plato's prophesy that democracies bankrupt themselves would be proven true.

By the end of 2000, Alan Greenspan found himself in another economic "pickle." Beginning in mid 1999 and ending in mid 2000, he had raised the fund rate from 4.75% to 6.5% attempting to slow the exploding stock market. This spooked investors and the market started tumbling downward. By years end, the NASDAQ had dropped 50%. The economy followed downward; a recession was on the horizon for 2001. To make matters worse, the surplus would disappear in 2001 as the plunging market took away all the stock option profits which meant lower capital gains tax revenues and a return to deficits.

Greenspan had to apply the usual medicine for recovery - fund rate decreases, seven in early 2001 alone. After the September 11 atrocity, as the recession deepened, unemployment rose and production dropped. Five more rate cuts followed ending up at 1.25% in October 2002 – the lowest rates since the 1950s. The rate went even lower to 1% in June 2003.

The expansive pressures on the economy were enormous during Bush's first term. Besides the easy credit supplied by the Federal Reserve, the first tax cut of $1.35 trillion (June 7, 2001), the second tax cut of $160 billion (May 28, 2003), and the emergency rebate of $600 per family ($40 billion total) poured billions into the economy. Added to that was the $60 billion transportation bill (December 2001) with $400 million in earmarks, the farm bill (May, 2002) with $250 billion in added subsidies, and then the prescription drug bill (November 25, 2003) costing the country $500 billion over ten years. An irresponsible Congress also added hundreds of millions of dollars in earmarks to these latter two bills.

If that wasn't enough expansion pressure, there were also the billion dollar costs of the Afghanistan and Iraq wars as well as the billions used to start up and run the new Homeland Security Agency. Just as Benjamin Harrison's Republican-controlled Congresses of his term (1889-93) were called the Billion Dollar Congresses for their spending extravagance, George Bush's could have easily been called the Trillion Dollar Congresses. During 2003 alone, the national debt rose $1.1 trillion, two trillion dollars higher than when Bush entered office. It would only get worse; the debt was $10.6 trillion when he left office in January 2009.

Alan Greenspan was chagrined that the Republicans had thrown fiscal restraint out the window. After all, they were supposed to be the fiscally responsible political party. But now they were acting like liberal Democrats - not caring about annual deficits, passing bill after bill to please various constituencies as a means of staying in political power.

Still, even with easy money and credit, the economy wasn't recovering as quickly as hoped after the dot.com stock crash and the ensuing recession. The economic pall that hung over the country after September 11th seemed to slow everything down. And it was only deepened when the Enron, Arthur Andersen and World Com corporate scandals surfaced in early December 2001. It wouldn't be until 2004 that economic activity started to pick up; the stock market led the way in 2003. Unfortunately, it had taken almost three years with the Federal fund rate near 1% to overcome the economic inertia. Those low rates would prove fateful for what was to come.

During the slow recovery years, helped along by the low rates, the housing market was undergoing a mini-boom. So active was the building and selling of homes that some financial writers were calling the housing boom the salvation of the entire economy. If they knew what was to follow from that housing activity, they would have never made those claims.

The post September 11th housing activity actually started during the euphoric atmosphere of the dot.com stock market bubble when everyone seemed to be making money (as well as the tax man) resulting in four years of budget surplus. This euphoria resulted in two economic movements – one the consumer housing market and the other, government deregulation of the finance industry – both leading to the financial collapse of 2008-2010 (probably longer).

With all the money floating around in the late 90s, the upscale consumer products market exploded. Luxury cars, yachts, jewelry, fine wines, expensive art and especially upscale homes and "McMansions" suddenly were in demand as the nouveau riche wanted everything...now! It was a classic inflation situation especially with homes as too much money was chasing too few homes. Home prices began to rise dramatically. Homebuilders, smelling the profits, began an equally dramatic increase in home building, especially McMansions. Home prices all over the country started to rise as homeowners realized that it was a seller's market. The nouveau riche wanted to spend, spend and spend!

Over in Congress, liberal Democrats were stifled in their social program plans for the surplus funds when President Clinton directed the funds to the Social Security program. They had thought the funds would be equally worthwhile to increase home ownership for the working class minorities. Perhaps with this in mind, Clinton appointed a new CEO for Fannie Mae, the quasi-government corporation that, along with Freddie Mac, were the country's biggest buyers and backers of mortgages. The implied mission of the new CEO was to make home ownership affordable and easier for people with poor credit, few assets and little or no money for a down payment.

The impetus for spreading home ownership to the lower classes really got going after the 2000-02 recession when the Fed fund rate hovered near one percent. Mortgage rates for a 15-year fixed-rate mortgage hit a low of 4.62% in June 2003. With the Federal government's encouragement and Fannie Mae and Freddie Mac buying up less-than-prime mortgages ("subprime"), the loan lending frenzy was on. The number of mortgage and loan brokers alone went up from around 50,000 in the mid 1990s to 136,000 in the mid 2000s (Bureau of Labor statistics). Everyone wanted some of that money even if it meant exploiting the financial ignorance of his or her customers or even their customer's greed.

Around the same time, the housing boom started (in the late 90s). Congress voted to allow another industry to fleece the public. Again the immediate cause was the millions being made on the dot.com stock market bubble. Banks, investment banks and insurance companies looked longingly at all the money stockbrokers and big investors were making on the market and wanted a piece of the action. Consequently, their lobbyists descended on Congress in 1999 to "persuade" them to change the 1933 Glass-Steagall Act that limited speculation in stocks and other investments, as well as preventing the merging of commercial and investment bank and insurance operations. The buzzwords were "globalization" and "modernization." US financial firms, it was argued, couldn't compete globally when other countries didn't have such restrictions. "Times have changed" the lobbyists maintained; the 1933 act was outmoded, behind the times. Globalization required modern financial methods. The modern financial institutions were very capable of regulating themselves they told Congress.

As usual, our inept Congress, very likely smelling generous campaign contributions for the upcoming 2000 Presidential campaign, voted overwhelmingly in a significant bipartisan count of 452-65 to repeal the most "onerous" restrictions of the "behind-the-times" Glass-Steagall Act. Indeed, the industry had already pumped some millions into campaign coffers between 1997 and November 1999. The Congressional members who voted for repeal actually accepted twice as much industry money as those who opposed the new law (Center for Responsible Politics). So it was business as usual between Congress and corporations – "you scratch my back and I'll scratch yours."

Robert Rubin, Clinton's former Treasury Secretary, was all for modernization as was Alan Greenspan. President Clinton, in the globalization camp since his signing of the NAFTA trade bill in 1993, readily signed the Financial Services Modernization Act.

Afterwards, the industry quickly sold it to the public as the convenient "one-stop financial services."

No one seemed to remember what happened some twelve years earlier when Congress deregulated the savings and loan industry in the mid 1980s at the lobbying request of the industry. Then, too, the S&L industry promised self-regulation while doling out generous campaign contributions. When the S&Ls went belly-up while self-regulating themselves a few years later, it cost the taxpayer $125 billion at the highest estimate.

If the Congress preferred not to remember the S&L deregulation debacle only twelve years prior, they were definitely not going to be reminded of the original reasons for passing the Glass-Steagall Act sixty-six years earlier. The 1920s were also a decade of modernization. Assembly line production of automobiles was revolutionizing manufacturing methods, radio was the wonderful new invention, airplane transportation was on the horizon and investment trusts were being heralded as the new financial innovation.

Instead of investors buying stock on their own, the investment trusts would sell its securities to the public in the form of stock, debentures and mortgage bonds and then use the proceeds to invest (usually in stocks), it all being touted as professional investment management to the public. Business knowledge, financial skill, even resident economists offering advice, brought in millions of dollars from little investors hoping to become rich. The miracle wealth production of the trusts really began when someone thought to "spin off" a subsidiary investment company and then the second one a third, and so forth until several or more interconnected investment trust companies were all held by the original company, all selling their own stock to the public and using the proceeds to invest in the stock market and in the stock of the original company, now considerably higher and rising as the market surged upwards. This interlocking pyramiding of investment trusts had a leveraging effect on all of them compounding the value of each and bringing in more millions of dollars as the investors were dazzled by the rocketing growth of the trusts.

Unfortunately, as soon as the market collapsed in 1929, so did the pyramids like a house of cards. With all their stock holdings and assets interconnected, if one trust collapsed so did the rest compounding the financial loss to the public. And that's why the

Glass-Steagall Act was passed originally – to protect the investor and eventually the taxpayer from just such a maze of interconnected investment companies that if one collapsed, they all did, intensifying the overall financial chaos. When investment banks are also allowed to engage in securities underwritings, buying and selling, the 1933 Congress thought that they couldn't be trusted to not overextend themselves in the pursuit of profit resulting eventually in a wide scale financial collapse whenever a financial interruption occurred. As subsequent events in 2007-08 showed, the 1999 Congress was wrong and the 1933 Congress was correct. There will always be new ways of doing things and new fiduciary instruments to make money but the greed of financiers remains the same.

Although the 106th Republican-controlled Congress did much damage to the country with its Finances Modernization Act, it wasn't finished in its ineptness. On October 30, 2000, just before the Presidential election, it passed another "modernization" bill, the Commodities Futures Modernization Act. This removed restrictions on outside interests (speculators) from buying futures in commodities such as corn, copper or oil in hopes of driving up prices to gain a profit. In essence, cornering the market for a commodity and then charging the highest price possible. At the same time, the Act deregulated the market for credit default swamps, a type of insurance against a commodity contract or security defaulting. These two "modernization" acts, financial services and commodities, would prove to be horrendous mistakes leading directly to the collapse of the financial system beginning in 2007.

It is of note that one of the biggest corporations lobbying to get commodity speculation restrictions removed was Enron whose CEO was a personal friend and large contributor to George Bush's Presidential campaign. As soon as the Act was passed, Enron bought large amounts of electricity futures effectively driving up the unit price for electricity in such states as California. The scheme was highly successful for Enron but it forced the local electrical companies to pass on the costs to outraged California consumers who eventually recalled a Democratic governor because of the high prices and installed a Republican in office.

The two "modernization" acts were clear cut examples of the Republican's Party bias against any governmental rules or regulations restricting what they see as an individual's (or company's) right to do anything they please in the business world. In that sense they have been the perfect ally of corporations, banks and businesses who deplore any restrictions on their "right" to make money almost since the Republic began.

For some inexplicable reason, the Republicans have always believed that CEOs bankers and businessmen are just as honest, with integrity as they themselves believe they are. But the historical record and the recent congressional and financial scandals of the Bush II years don't back up this belief. Given the opportunity, these so-called honest people have historically cut every corner, devised every scheme and pushed the legality to the edge to acquire as much wealth as they could without regard to the consequences impacting the country and its workers. More will be said later about these "honest" persons.

With the collapse of the dot.com stock market in 2000-01, the smart investors and speculators sold their holdings early for huge profits and dallied with "shorting" other stocks in the down-plunging market for more profit before moving their money into the next "hot" arena – the soon-to-be booming mortgage market. Eyeing the profits that Fannie Mae and Freddie Mac were making in this market, the Wall Street investment banks (no longer restricted from buying or selling securities because of the Finances Modernization Bill) began competing with Mae and Mac buying up the mortgage loans that were returning 6-8% returns in a post September 11th economy where the Fed fund rate was near one percent.

It is at this juncture that the two paths leading to the 2008 financial collapse, the mortgage loan frenzy and the government's accommodating deregulation of financial services, merged. Given the favorable returns in a down economy, billions of dollars poured into the mortgage market, a $17 trillion market of which $12 trillion were subprime loans. The figures were huge as were the prospects for profit especially when someone (probably an investment banker) had the bright idea of packaging a hundred or so mortgage loans together and selling them to investors, banks, foreign countries (even small towns in Norway), state retirement funds, university endowments, foundations, corporate retirement funds, labor pension funds, etc. Anyone who had money and wanted a relatively high steady income were targets once the financial restrictions were repealed for investment banks, banks and insurance companies thanks to the 106th Congress and

President Clinton. There was no impediment for the financial industry to pile up the profits to be generously distributed to company officers as bonuses, some as high as $50 million to CEOs.

Another clever idea was the mixing up of prime mortgages with subprime mortgages in the mortgage security package to spread the risk as well as to utilize the more risky subprime mortgage. If they were sold separately at the going returns, investors would pick the less-risky prime loans over the more risky subprime ones. These new packages were called Collateralized Debt Obligations (CDOs).

To further assuage investors about the safety of the CDOs, the bond rating companies were asked to grade them. For a $250,000 fee for a batch of CDOs, the bond rating companies were happy to take on the business. So much, in fact, that the CEOs pressured their analysts to give the CDOs the highest grade possible – AAA. Without a history of reference for such securities, the poor analysts had no basis to give any ratings at all. It would only be a guesstimate if they did. The CEOs insisted; some honest analysts quit in disgust but others (to keep their jobs) gave the high rating to the CDOs even though they all contained very risky subprime loans. In the end, the CEOs got their ratings, the ratings companies made billions, and millions in bonuses were rewarded. The investment banks peddling the CDOs were overjoyed. Talk about fraud!

A still further clever scheme to make money on the mortgage securities was the selling of credit default swaps by insurance companies who promised to pay the full price of the security to the investor in the event of a default on the security. This form of insurance was supposed to remove all risk for the purchaser of mortgage securities. If some of the risky mortgages in the CDOs did go into default, the other prime mortgages in the package would theoretically offset the defaults. And if a lot of the mortgages defaulted wiping out the value of the entire package, the wise investor who bought a credit default swap on the package could get the full value of the security paid by the insurance company.

With hefty fees involved, the insurance companies eagerly sought the new business. In fact, without any reserve restrictions, thanks again to the 106th Congress and Clinton repealing all credit swap default regulations, the companies could sell trillions of dollars worth of swaps which they did without having to even think about having enough reserves to pay claims in the event of a major financial collapse, which, of course, is exactly what happened leaving the taxpayers bailing out insurance companies to the tune of billions of dollars. They got the bonuses and we got the shaft. Millions of us are losing our homes and our jobs.

It's not all the fault of the 106th Congress, Clinton or Alan Greenspan. The Wall Street federal regulators, the Security Exchange Commission (another 1930s enactment by a wise Congress) seem to have accommodated the financial industry in its greedy quest for more profit and bonuses in the Bush years. In April 2004, just as the subprime frenzy was getting up a head of steam, the SEC regulators heard the same old refrain from the big investment banks, government restrictions were making them noncompetitive in the global financial markets. They desperately needed a relaxation of the reserve requirements in relation to debt or they would have to cut back operations and that would jeopardize jobs. The demand to purchase mortgage loans as a means to create more CDOs was so competitive that individual mortgage prices were going up and up so that the investment banks had to borrow more money from the commercial banks. But they were already at or near the legal debt-to-asset ratio of about 15-1. The "loss of jobs" remark always perked up the ears of Bush-appointed regulators. Approval of the industry's request immediately followed. This meant that billions of dollars of reserves meant to cushion any losses were effectively freed up to buy more mortgages and create more profitable securities. The banks could also borrow billions more "if they needed to." Apparently Bear Stearns Investment Bank did just that. When they collapsed in March 2008, their debt-to-asset ratio was 33-1.

Critics say that this quiet meeting in April 2004 between the bankers and the SEC was the "tipping point" (another current buzz term) for the whole fiscal mess. The floodgates were opened and mountains of debt and mortgages poured into Wall Street. If the SEC had said "No" to lowering the legal reserves, the great financial scam might have been choked off there and then. As it was, the investment banks, banks, insurance companies and security rating companies went merrily on their way for almost four more years taking in the profits and freely dishing out obscene salaries, stock options and bonuses.

All that money came from investors who trusted the investment banks, the AAA ratings on the securities and the SEC regulators who never blew the whistle on these irresponsible companies nor their executives. Indeed, after the 2007-08 collapse, reports surfaced that said the SEC seemed to purposely look the other way at all these financial maneuvers. It was exactly this type of interconnected financial dealings by greedy corporations and executives that the 1933 Glass-Steagall Act was passed to prevent. Instead, the country's bulwark against greedy financial dealings was destroyed by a corrupt 106th Congress more interested in campaign dollars and their own jobs than the financial wellness of the country, by an incredibly naïve President and by the country's leading economist who should have known better.

To be fair, Alan Greenspan and Bush officials did appear before Congress in 2004 and 2005 warning that Freddie Mac and Fannie Mae were taking on so much mortgage debt ($5 trillion), any reversal in their future could take down the entire financial system. Their caution was met by vilification from the liberal Democrats advocating "affordable housing" as a mean and racist attempt to deprive minorities of owning their own homes.

If Alan Greenspan sensed the growing danger of the huge subprime mortgage bubble, he probably also sensed that it was too late to deflate it without plunging the country into another recession or even a depression. He knew the history of trying to stop a boom at its height. The 2000-02 recession started shortly after the Fed fund rate was raised in 1998-99. The same thing happened in 1987 when the Fed tightened credit just before the October stock market collapse that led eventually to the 1989-91 recession. And in 1920 when the Federal Reserve Board abruptly raised the discount rate, a two-year depression followed. Far better to retire from the Fed in 2006 with dignity intact just when the subprime entanglements started to unravel than be tarred and feathered with the inevitable crash just over the horizon.

A tough regulatory bill seeking to rein in Fannie Mae and Freddie Mac sponsored by four Republican Senators in 2005 never became law partly because of the liberal Democrats opposing it and mostly because of an intense covert lobbying campaign against the bill and the Republican Senators, paid for by Mac and Mae to the tune of several million dollars. Their CEOs and other officers were making millions in bonuses so every attempt was made to keep the big bucks flowing.

The eventual collapse of Freddie Mac and Fannie Mae is a prime example of how congressional members refuse to take any responsibility for their previous self-serving acts leading to such collapses. In the first half of the decade, the Democratic liberals pushed for lower lending standards for the poor and minorities; in 2008 after the collapse, the same Democrats as committee heads are sanctimoniously investigating the "culprits" of the Great Collapse of 2008. Everybody except themselves will be fingered.

One more financial debacle of 2008 can be blamed on the 106th Congress. Their repealing of the restriction on outside speculation on food, energy, metal and oil commodities written in the Commodities Exchange Act of 1936 led directly to $4 a gallon gas prices in the summer of 2008. As mentioned, when the dot.com stock market collapsed in 2000, investors switched their money to the mortgage loan boom post 9/11. When that boom started to collapse in 2007, the investment money moved to commodities that were no longer regulated against speculation. Big investment banks started buying large amounts of future contracts for themselves and customers in oil, corn, wheat and rice hoping to drive up the price and make a big killing. The price of a barrel of oil surged upwards near $150 a barrel and was projected to hit $200 by the end of 2008. Four dollar a gallon gas immediately followed almost reducing SUV sales to zero and jeopardizing the health of the automobile makers whom the taxpayers had to eventually bail out. Congressional investigators were told by the investment banks that the rise in prices was due to supply and demand, their usual lie. All summer long, OPEC had said the oil price surge was due to speculators but no one in the US wanted to believe them. As was noted afterwards, demand for oil was dropping in 2008 and supply increasing so there was no way that the high price was due to supply and demand.

At the same time, world food prices were rising so high that many countries and their people could no longer afford to feed themselves. All this worldwide misery because a corrupt US Congress opened the gates to commodity speculation by greedy Wall Streeters.

While greedy Wall Streeters have always been involved in financial crises, they couldn't have been if our inept Congresses, Presidents and the Federal Reserve Board hadn't provided the means by creating financially expansive periods or by repealing protective laws for their own self-serving reasons.

If the American voter has any intelligence at all, in 2010 they would vote out of office any remaining member of the 106th Congress (still campaigning) who had voted for the "modernization" of the financial services and commodity markets. Not only that but the voter should ask themselves if it was worthwhile for the liberal Democrats to push for lowering mortgage lending practices to favor creditless home buyers. This aided the financial system collapse of 2007-08 that has made the lives of the poor and minorities even more stressful.

As we have seen now after examining some two hundred years of US recessions and depressions, every expansive period is always followed by a contractive period that results in unemployment and economic malaise. George Bush's expansive policies were no different. The events on September 11, 2001 and corporate scandals slowed his policy's effects for a few years but very low Federal fund rates, earlier finance regulation repeals by Congress, a Democratic push for minority home ownership and the SEC's decision to lower investment bank reserve requirements all merged to intensify the expansion resulting in the biggest contraction perhaps in the history of the country. With final figures probably not available for several years, unemployment is already nearing 10 million in mid 2009. The national debt at the end of 2008 stood at $9.6 trillion, up from $5.6 trillion in 2000. With the bailout of the financial and mortgage markets (expected to exceed $2 trillion or more the next two years), the national debt will have almost tripled in just ten years.

In 1930, the national debt stood at $16 billion; 78 years later it was $9.6 trillion, probably going up to $12 trillion by 2010. These latest huge figures mean that the government has had to essentially print $12 trillion to cover the annual deficits in tax revenue in order to maintain the daily functioning of the country as well as to pay for wars, social welfare programs, natural disasters and recessions and depressions (of their own making). How is this possible that in a supposedly wealth-producing capitalistic economy, we're not even paying our own way? Well, one major reason is the constant cutting of taxes promised by Presidential candidates in order to get elected. With an electorate that always votes its pocketbook rather than its intelligence (if there is any), the end result after 78 years of deficit spending is an outrageous $12 trillion national debt.

Of course, even if the country had a higher, stable tax income that would be intended to minimize annual deficits or even produce a balanced budget (heaven forbid!), 78 years of inept, profligate Congresses have clearly shown that more tax income would merely be doled out to the public as social welfare programs disguised as altruistic necessities but really are political necessities to win votes and keep politicians' jobs.

When one thinks of the enormous amounts of economic misery the country has suffered because of deficit spending in the form of unemployment, inflation, middle-class wage stagnation and a lower standard of living for millions, one has to ask: "Isn't there a better way?"

Franklin Roosevelt used John Maynard Keynes' deficit spending theories in the manner that Keynes advocated: in emergency conditions of economic depression to get the system going again to restore prosperity and employment. But even Roosevelt would probably have been disturbed to see Presidents Kennedy and Johnson use deficit spending to stimulate a more or less normal, slow-growing economy. The liberal economic advisors to Kennedy weren't content with the 2-3% growth of the Eisenhower years; they wanted 4-5%, maybe even 6%, to reflect well on their advice and with the voters in the next election. To be sure as we have seen, LBJ's tax cut and Great Society welfare programs did indeed produce 5% growth in the years immediately following but the long-term results of the expansive sixties was twelve years of an inflationary roller coaster, mini-recessions, and unemployment starting in 1970.

Regardless of the long-term negative results of deficit spending, Roosevelt's legacy appealed to politicians of both parties. It was a sure-fire way to get elected without being blamed for the five to ten year down-the-line negative effects. They counted on the voters' poor memories. And they sure weren't going to stand up with a mea culpa speech if they wanted to keep their cushy jobs.

It can be argued that just as the mindset of deficit spending invaded the political world, it also invaded the country's life style. Beginning around 1984, the US personal savings rate began to decline: almost 11% then, by 2006 it was -1%. At the same time, the consumers' credit card debt began to rise. Much of this can be attributed to the fact that middle-class income stagnation also began in the 80s but if government could live beyond its means (in debt year after year without stigma), why not the average citizen? An entire generation has grown up accepting debt as the norm in their lives. Indeed, using debt is the only means possible to maintain a lifestyle of instant gratification.

Proponents of deficit spending are reluctant to criticize it, going out of their way to blame inflation, recurrent recessions and unemployment on everything but the historical fact that deficit spending produces economic expansion followed by psychological contraction, leading to unemployment increases.

Even proponents recognize, however, that if the annual deficits adding up to a national debt even greater than $12 trillion, devaluing the dollar even more, then at some point other countries will stop accepting the increasingly worthless dollar, stop buying our debt, and allow us to collapse into a second rate nation with a decidedly lower living standard.

History says ancient Rome collapsed with the barbaric Germanic tribes overrunning the empire and sacking its cities in the 5th Century AD. But Rome's internal economic system had been collapsing for centuries with productivity falling along with tax income while the welfare dole increased to the point that eventually the Roman currency became so worthless that even the army wouldn't accept it. Without an army to protect its borders, ancient Rome disappeared from history. An empire or a democracy is only as strong as its currency. Devalue it with continuous deficit spending and then dissolution of the society and the nation is the likely eventuality.

Chapter Eleven

Conclusions

"... economic contractions happen and are a natural phenomenon." Those words were written by a businessman trying to assuage the public that the current 2008-09 recession is just another natural occurrence that we shall soon exit from just as we did all the previous natural recessions.

It is difficult to believe that a businessman, of all occupations, would write those words let alone believe them. The main purpose of this book is to refute that very myth. Contractions aren't a natural occurrence like the seasons coming around every year. They are man made, generated by the Federal government's actions, by Presidents, by corrupt Congresses or by an inept Federal Reserve Board.

As we have seen, there are three phases to these economic disasters beginning with the expansion phase whereby the government provides easy money and credit either by a tax cut, social welfare program expenditures, low Federal fund rates, repeal of financial regulatory laws or by several other means. Whichever is used, the motivation is almost always the politician's desire to ingratiate themselves with the voters to get elected or to ingratiate themselves with banks and corporations in quest of generous campaign contributions. This first phase can also be called the enabling phase because it sets up "easy money" financial conditions enabling the sharp operators, speculators, exploiters and even cheats to quickly make money.

Alan Greenspan's memorable phrase "irrational exuberance" can be used to describe the moneymaking second phase. John Kenneth Galbraith might have called it the "euphoria phase." In either case, the various operators et al. listed above take the opportunity afforded by the Federal government to make hay, so to speak. The 2001-08 cycle is a good example of the operators et al. in action as well as the government's enabling actions. Encouraged by liberal Democrats to make home loans to anyone breathing, the mortgage brokers and lenders cheated and exploited the elderly, minorities and the poor while the too-low Federal fund rates guaranteed millions of trusting and eager customers. The congressional repealing of financial regulations and the SEC lowering of legal reserves for banks enabled investment banks to create unregulated, extremely profitable mortgage-backed securities that were fraudulently rated AAA and sell them worldwide as low-risk investments. When the mortgages went into default, the entire interconnected financial system collapsed.

The third phase, of course, is the contraction one in which credit dries up, productivity plunges, workers become unemployed and a psychological malaise engulfs our country and the world. Think about it: the government enables operators, speculators, exploiters and cheats to make billions while we, the little people, lose our jobs, our homes, our dreams and our belief in America. In his book in 1759 *The Theory of Moral Sentiments* (Adam Smith, 1723-1790), the "father" of capitalism, comments on the preferential treatment the rich received from government: "Government is initiated for the defense of the rich against the poor and therefore they should be taxed progressively on their income and property."

In essence, for over a hundred and fifty years the government has enabled the rich to get richer, and the poor, poorer. It has been a giant con game as the Congress became more corrupt and the money amounts involved, larger. The country started as a republic, changed to a democracy because of populist pressure and is now a corporate oligarchy posing as a democracy. Ben Franklin is said to have responded to the question: Is the new country a monarchy or a republic? His answer: "A republic but it's up to you to keep it." Unfortunately, we haven't.

But the little people, the voters, aren't blameless in this transformation. After all, it is they who vote the increasingly corrupt politicians into office election after election. It is they who accept the politicians' bribes leading to expansions and later contractions. They, who value tax cuts and earmarks over integrity and frugality, are the first culprits in eroding the government.

Nevertheless, even if ignorant voters have to reap what they have sown, the severe penalty of job and home loss with each expansion or contraction cycle is way out of proportion to the operators, speculators and cheats who feast on the public during the expansion years and weather the contraction with income and home intact. Drastic reforms are necessary to stop this outrageous con game once and for all!

The Founding Fathers knew only too well the corruptibility of men as evidenced by their deliberate check and balance design of the new government as well as their Bill of Rights. But as remarkable men as they were, they couldn't be expected to envision all the future corruption in being elected to office and in keeping the office, nor in the unimaginable amounts of money involved in elections.

The 2007-08 financial collapse is clear evidence that reform is needed in our political process and corporate governance. Not just reluctant, patchwork reform as in the past but DRASTIC REFORM meaning Constitutional amendment reform to insure that the political and financial future of the country is stable, frugal and strong.

Losing jobs and homes in a contraction is the utmost debilitating result not only for the individual but also for the country. The only way to avoid such horrendous results is with a long-term stable economy in which expected standards are followed – no surprises, no instigated dangerous expansions upsetting the psychology of stable behavior.

Federal Reserve Reform The historical record clearly shows that since its first operation in 1914, the Federal Reserve has been deeply involved in every depression or recession the country has suffered. Indeed, it has been the primary culprit in most of them, either 1) in generating extended "easy money" periods by keeping the interest rates too low for too long or by purchasing open market securities excessively. These policies have always produced a booming economy and stock market only to inevitably implode into a financial collapse, or 2) triggering an actual collapse by raising the interest rates too fast or too high.

Such historical, monumental ineptitude calls loudly for reform. Some critics such as the Libertarian Congressman from Texas Ron Paul, want to abolish the Fed and reestablish the gold standard for economic stability. (In 1971, President Nixon severed our last ties to the gold standard when, in response to our foreign creditors who demanded payment in gold as our high inflation rates devalued the dollar, ended the gold payment policy permanently). It should be remembered that the gold standard offered no protection against economic depressions in the decades before the advent of the Fed. Presidents and Congresses were still able to generate "easy money" times through various means.

Any reform of the Fed should stop them from manipulating the interest rates and open market security purchases to generate "easy money." It should be restricted to its original mandate of accommodating the credit needs of commerce and provide for stability in currency and prices. In other words, economic stability was the prime goal of the original proponents of the Fed. It has done just the opposite. In the current crisis, it looked the other way when banks got "too big to fail;" it ignored, along with the Securities Exchange Commission, the introduction of clever new financial instruments; it allowed bank debt to dangerously outweigh assets...in short, all the bank oversight necessary to maintain economic stability was replaced by a naïve belief in bankers' self-regulation. Any reform should be directed towards close oversight of the banking system, preventing practices that will lead to economic collapse instead of always trying to cleanup the mess afterwards. A proactive rather than a reactive policy.

Government Reform Economic stability also has to begin with drastic changes including Constitutional amendments in politics. The first change should be the removal of financial responsibility from Congress. Their historical fiscal record has been atrocious as evidenced by the too-many recessions and depressions the country has endured not to mention the stultifying current national debt. The Founding Fathers believed that the safest place for the nation's financial security would be in the hands of the elected representatives. They didn't see their self-serving tactics, utter lack of frugality, or their absence of integrity.

In place of the House handling the country's finances, a Federal Economics Board (FEB) should be established working in conjunction with the Federal Reserve Board to maintain long-term economic stability. Instead of "yes men" economic advisors, the President should appoint six academic economists to the Board. Three with a liberal bias, three conservative, the equal ideologies meant to force a compromise decision on policies good for the economy rather than an ideological one for the benefit of politicians and their parties. Their tenures should be for life, similar to the Supreme Court, to keep the Board as separate as possible from politics. Their mission should be a long-term stable economy catching in the bud any expansive tendencies that could lead to a destructive contraction negatively affecting employment – the ultimate life force of any economy.

This change, of course, would require a major Constitutional amendment that Congress would never allow unless populist pressure became so great as to jeopardize the politician's job. Even then it would need a strong President leading the way.

With that in mind, the Board's first duty would be to oversee a complete ban on any Federal political candidate promising a tax cut. Instead of the up and down tax rates with each succeeding administration, a long-term tax rate set by the Board (say for 25 years) would allow the public and business just what to expect in taxes. Knowing what to expect is a factor of stability. Setting the top rate at 25% for incomes over $1 million for 25 years without any deductions, loopholes or credits (for all tax levels) might bring a sense of probity to the government and financial circles. At the same time, a steady stream of tax revenues might allow a gradual pay down of the national debt.

Equally necessary for stability would be to keep in check the historically fiscally irresponsible Congress by vetting every social program act for amount and time of expenditures. Lyndon Johnson's zeal for adulation and votes resulted in a large tax cut combined with huge Great Society program expenditures all being injected into the economy at the same time. This destabilized the economy and subjected the country to a twelve-year aftermath of periodic inflation, recession and job loss.

A further necessary check on Congress would be a balanced budget Constitutional amendment ending the fiscal foolishness of deficit spending on a permanent basis rather than only in economic emergencies as Keynes meant it to be. It can be agreed that the lack of a balanced budget requirement in the Constitution is the most ominous omission in the entire document. The Founding Fathers, with the mindset of their times in avoiding debt, probably never dreamed that future politicians would use debt in such a cavalier manner. In times of dire emergencies, of course, the balanced budget policy would have to be waived for a finite period.

To make Congress even more fiscally responsible, a Constitutional amendment limiting their terms in office is extremely necessary: two terms for Senators and six years for Representatives. Again, Congress would fight tooth and nail to keep their cushy jobs as long as they can bamboozle ignorant voters. The usual argument against such a proposal is that more years in office provides experience and makes the system more efficient. This is so transparently a self-serving myth that it doesn't deserve repudiation. The only experience long-serving politicians gather is how to hide their earmarks more effectively, have more of them, and how to command more generous campaign contributions from corporations, unions and other interest groups. According to Alan Greenspan (ibid.), earmarks increased from 3,023 in 1995 to 16,000 in 2005. This robbed the taxpayers of tens of billions of dollars.

Corporate Reform While a Federal Economics Board would oversee the stability of the economy and check a notorious spendthrift Congress, the Federal Reserve Board would look after the financial stability of the country meaning the close regulation of commercial banks, investment banks, insurance companies and corporations in general. Perhaps the first requirement for this oversight is for the Reserve Board to get rid of the naïve mindset once and for all that self-regulation works for these operators. They have shown repeatedly throughout the economic history of the country that they can't be trusted. Judge them by their deeds, not their words.

Secondly, the Board should command the Congress to reinstate all the financial protection laws that the bipartisan 106th Congress repealed. In addition, reserve requirements for these financial companies should be restored to double the amount required before the Securities Exchange Commission lowered the requirements in 2004. Further, the Board should vet all new operations and fiduciary instruments such as hedge fund operations, mortgage lending practices, derivatives, mortgage-backed securities and credit default swaps, all used in recent expansions to swindle investors and tax payers.

To prevent future expansions and contractions, both Boards should demand of Congress that all lobbying for profit be declared a Federal offense with a twenty-year jail sentence and a $5 million fine (more for corporations). Just declaring some bills are off limits to lobbyists as President Obama recently did will not work. Lobbyists are already boasting that they will go around Obama's ban and become more secretive. A permanent "making-it-a-crime" with severe penalties is the only option left to get rid of our corporate oligarchy.

In conjunction with that aim, no corporate contributions to political candidates should be allowed at all. Only individual contributions should be allowed based on the public funding programs in Maine and Arizona and with no op-out option for any candidate. An amendment to the Bill of Rights Free Speech clause would be required for these corporate restrictions. Unfortunately, integrity can't be regulated but political and financial manipulators can be if we have the will. It will be well worth it if future contractions can be avoided and workers allowed to keep their jobs and homes because we do have the common sense and will. The country has gone through 150 years of outright swindles generated by corrupt politicians and clever financiers. It is time it stopped!

Stock Market Reform Which brings us to the stock market, the biggest swindle of all. Lucky Luciano, the notorious mafia mob boss of some sixty years ago, when taking a tour of the New York Stock Exchange and seeing the floor specialist's operations, was reported to have muttered: "I've been in the wrong racket" (Ney, 1970). And racket it is. For over one hundred years, stock market specialists who handle stock trades have been ripping off investors by manipulating stock price, timing of trades and short selling to make a profit for themselves and their firms over and above regular handling commissions. After the 1929 crash, Congress, under strong pressure from the press and the public, constructed a strong regulatory Securities and Exchange Act in 1934. Unfortunately, it was gutted by administration officials favorable to the stock exchange.

John T. Flynn, a financial columnist writing in *The New Republic* on May 9, 1934, laments the gutting of the pending bill (Ney, 1970).

> "Will Wall Street and the racketeering banks...which have robbed countless thousands of trusting depositors and investors through these predatory and unconscionable affiliates, succeed in getting away with this? I predict they will...They have succeeded in taking out of the Stock Exchange Bill almost every important tooth designed to bite into Wall Street...The most successful raids on the bill were engineered by men in the Federal Reserve Board, the Treasury and the Department of Commerce..."

The robbery still goes on. In 2006, the New York Stock Exchange and seven specialist firms were sued by the California

Public Workers Pension Fund alleging that the exchange actively participated with the specialists in wide-ranging manipulative, self-serving, deceptive trading thereby misleading investors on the integrity of the exchange and its specialists. Apparently the specialists committed thousands of illegal trades always for their own profit or for preferred customers. This resulted in millions of dollars lost to public investors. The Security Exchange Commission only fined each firm $35 million and allowed them to continue operating. The NY Stock Exchange relationship with the SEC has always been as a partner rather than a regulatory adversary. They have always posed to the public as an agency of integrity and strong oversight while working hand-in-glove with the exchange behind the scenes (Ney, 1970).

The role of specialists in matching up buy-and-sell orders and establishing a price has largely been replaced by computers for smaller trade but they have still hung on to large block trading with large fee profits. To avoid altogether, however, the inherent conflict in interest between their role as brokers handling trades for customers and traders for their own profitable accounts, the specialist should be abolished, letting computers handle all trades. Many think a less volatile and more honest market would be the result.

Until the stock market becomes honest and fair, economically ignorant workers should be advised to put their retirement funds into much safer US Treasury notes and bonds or municipal bonds. The interest earned is much smaller compared to a stock market high-flyer stock but how many of those are there? Not many, and don't believe the stock exchange propaganda of a 10% return on stocks over a number of years. The Dow Jones average at the end of 2008 stood near 8000 just as it did in 1998. If you were the average retirement fund investor and let your stocks ride for your later retirement, your gross return would be near or at zero for the last ten years. However, if you panicked (out of economic ignorance) and sold your stocks in the market plunges of 2002 and 2008, you would have lost 40-50% of your retirement funds. That would apply to the earlier plunge in October 1987 also.

Another standard bit of stock exchange propaganda is the "diversify for safety" one which is really a clever (deceitful?) way to get you to buy more stocks. In any plunge of the market, all stocks drop in price no matter how diverse or how many you own. That is clearly evident in the $10 trillion in value the market lost in the plunge between October 2007 and November 2008. So, investing in Treasury notes or bonds won't make you a millionaire but you will have a safe, growing bottom line for retirement as well as keeping all of your money in the next crash.

The last three market crashes – 1987, 2000, 2008 – should demonstrate clearly to the public that the Republican idea of putting part of one's Social Security tax into the stock market is sheer lunacy, if not outright deceitful. It would mean billions for the financial industry buddies of the Republican Party and zilch for the investor in the next crash.

As a corollary to more strict regulation of corporations and the stock exchange, the practice of stock options should be abolished. It's a major factor in the income inequality that is today dividing classes – a 40-1 ratio previously and now over 400-1 between CEOs and the average worker's income. Also, with stock options, a corporate CEO's main concern is no longer corporate products, marketing and income but rather the price of the company's stock affecting the ultimate price of his or her own stock options. The focus on stock price is so intense that corporations such as Enron and Health South cooked the books to make Wall Street think the companies were growing strongly thereby keeping the stock price up for more millions when the options were exercised.

Critics maintain that stock exchanges and their markets are nothing but crooked gambling casinos, their main operation being to fleece the financially ignorant public. They point out that while Initial Public Offerings (IPO) in the market do provide startup funds for new companies, it's the insiders – company officials, underwriting banks, venture capitalists, preferred clients – who make the big bucks selling their millions of shares to the public after an artificial price rise orchestrated by the specialists has taken place. There are many alternative sources of startup money today – commercial banks, investment banks, insurance companies, venture capitalists, state retirement funds – but that would mean the insiders would actually be investing in the possible long-term success of a new company rather than in the sure thing of immediate big bucks of public money. And with stock market crashes always dragging the economy down, the critics think we would be better off without the exchanges.

Predatory Operators With the numerous recurring recessions and depressions in the financial history of the United States, one has to wonder if the politicians and bankers are capable of learning anything from those past episodes. The most recent (2007-2010?) collapse emphatically says they are not. This appears most likely because of the character traits they display. They seem to be possessed with an innate sense of superiority, spending their entire lives trying to prove it to their peers and to themselves. They are aggressive, competitive, egotistical, and even arrogant. They have their own relativistic moral code. Rules and regulations are for others. In their zeal to get elected or to make money, they will cut any corner, get any edge, make any barely-legal or barely-ethical deal to acquire the prize. They view money and power as badges of their superiority. Consequently, they enter the realm of high finance where money, power and prestige can be had or go into politics where power and prestige (money on the side) are the goals. Adam Smith (ibid.) had this to say about politicians: "Successful politicians are arrogant, presumptuous, great admirers of themselves (and show) great contempness [sic] of other people."

They also are impulsive and incautious using daring-do and risk-taking to demonstrate their superiority. Extravagant spending on luxury items and mansions are also means of displaying superiority, an outer scorecard (to use the financier Warren Buffet's term) to impress others as opposed to an inner scorecard of achievements kept personal and understated with modest individuals. In every expansion/contraction cycle, it is this type of immodest, aggressive person that is involved to the fullest, bringing about economic misery for the rest of America.

The liberal iconoclastic economist Thorstein Veblen recognized these predatory operators when, in 1899, he published his classic book *The Theory of the Leisure Class* in which he referred to them as "exploiters" of society in making their money. Like the predatory operators who detest menial labor, Veblen's leisure class found manual work "irksome." He thought the type was descended genetically from barbarian tribal warriors and later feudal warlords and their warrior henchmen. So these "superior" beings have always been with us and always will be. Indeed, since WWII they seem to be increasing in number relative to we "inferior" types in the US judging from the decrease in civility, the need for instant gratification, the widespread ostentatious materialism and the rapacious frenzy to get rich.

Veblen's leisure class not only thought their superiority was responsible for their acquiring riches but resorted to modifying Charles Darwin's (1809-82) biological premise "survival of the adaptive" to Herbert Spencer's (1820-1903) pseudo-philosophical premise "survival of the fittest" as justification for their "obscene riches" of the time. Some went even further seeing God's work in the natural selection of superior men to construct and lead industrial and financial complexes capable of hiring the poor as a benefit to all of society. John D. Rockefeller (1839-1937), the oil industry Robber Baron, was quoted as saying: "This is not an evil tendency in business. It is merely the working out of a law of nature and a law of God" (Mason, 1965, p. 579).

Today, the predatory operators leave the philosophizing to others and use more subtle methods to justify their existence. Relying on their own propensity for risk taking, they have propagandized Congress and the country into thinking that risk taking is a necessary requirement for capitalism and they should not be judged too harshly if the risks fail. However the very existence of the financier Warren Buffet, one of the two richest men in America (the computer entrepreneur Bill Gates the other), contradicts that myth completely. Buffet is a modest, cautious, frugal, conscientious investor who goes out of his way to avoid investment risk and is completely opposite from the devious politician or the rapacious predatory operator. Gates is a real example of capitalism at its best building a business from scratch and giving thousands lucrative jobs.

Another propaganda myth favored by the financial operators and politicians is the one declaring that a 3-5% high growth rate for the economy is necessary to promote jobs and optimism in the population to give them a sense of progress in their lives. This mindset is sheer nonsense growing out of the predator's need to reinforce their sense of superiority. How better than to point to growth rates of 3-5% as being the result of their "mastery" in the business world? Politicians, too, use the high growth mindset as a means to getting re-elected. "We got the economy moving again – remember that folks when you go to the polls."

In reality, a high growth rate means more profits for the rich and less for the workers. Even though economic growth in the US from WWII on has been high, the wages of the average worker has stagnated or even retreated over this period while the income of the rich has exploded upwards. One recent study (Richard

Douthwaite, 1992, *The Growth Illusion,* Council Oak Books, Tulsa, OK) indicates the higher the growth rate, the lower the social progress for the worker.

There is nothing wrong with a steady growth rate of 1% or less. Indeed, it would provide price and wage stability not to mention avoiding inflation, job and home loss that has always followed when an expansive high growth rate degenerates into a contractive recession. In economics, as in the fable, the tortoise's slow pace always wins out over the hare's fast pace. Warren Buffet's steady, less risky, long-term investment versus the fast buck lure of mortgage-backed securities wins out in the end.

Criminals When John Flynn wrote the words "...the racketeering banks...which have robbed countless thousands..." in his May 9, 1934 financial column in *The New Republic* describing the culprits of the 1929 stock market crash, he could have been writing about the culprits of the 2007-10(?) financial collapse. For they too were engaged in racketeering, involving a scheme to rob investors by selling them fraudulently rated securities. What difference is there in a petty thief robbing a citizen by pretending to have a gun in his pocket or a predatory operator robbing an investor by pretending a security is top rated?

If the "blue collar" petty robber is caught, he'll probably end up in jail. If the "white collar" robber were ever caught, it would be a surprise. Already in New York financial circles, apologists are questioning whether any bank or corporate officer is clearly guilty of anything illegal. And how, they ask, could any guilty person (if there are any) be located among the hundreds of executives working on Wall Street or among the thousands of mortgage lenders around the country?

The answer to that is first to recognize and admit that a crime harming millions of people has been committed. The second is to investigate the top three executives – the CEO, CFO, COO – of every company that either needed taxpayer bailout money or collapsed completely. Countrywide Finances, Fannie Mae, Freddie Mac, Lehman Brothers, AIG, Citibank and Standard & Poor come to mind. The top three executives should have known where the profits were coming from. They were, after all, quick to accept outrageous bonuses for their "expert" managing. There should be some criminal indictments when trillions of dollars of bailout money are necessary to keep the crooked maze afloat.

Furthermore, the investigations shouldn't be meaningless. Congressional hearings or SEC probes are usually conducted to salve the media and the public until the uproar dies down and all is forgotten without any remedial action. Indeed, both the Congress and the SEC aided and abetted the swindle by passing legislation favorable to the swindlers, at their own lobbying request no less. So the Congress and the SEC should also be investigated for being criminal accomplices preferably by the Justice Department or an outside ethics board. Congresses in-house Ethics Committee is a joke and is one more example that predatory operators can't be trusted to regulate themselves.

A political cartoon by Ed Stein appearing in the summer of 2009 perfectly sums up the economic callousness that has plagued our country since its inception. On the left, in a Wall Street high rise office is a group of investment bankers happily toasting with champagne the return of multimillion dollar bonuses, singing "happy days" again, while in the street below, silhouetted against the New York backdrop, is a line of downcast, unemployed waiting to enter the unemployment office.

There, in a simple cartoon without need of words, Stein has portrayed the eternal economic problem: predatory operators without one iota of empathy for the jobless "wretches" below them. If words were necessary, they could have been: "We've got ours, the hell with you!"

There is no doubt that capitalism is the best system to provide economic incentive and wealth but it is also the worst system to allow aggressive abuse and disparity in an economy. The problem for any capitalistic society is how to compensate for the varieties in human nature but not destroy incentive and wealth production as communism does.

For free capitalism to work properly, the participants – entrepreneurs, businessmen and bankers – must be honest, with integrity and a sense of justice. If the government has to step in with regulations to provide as much honesty as possible in the system, then the above participants have only themselves to blame. The mere fact that government has had to consistently intrude upon the system, imposing rules, clearly shows that the participants have been "gaming" the system for their own financial advantage. Such actions are not capitalism but rather thievery, stealing from investors and consumers, leading to destruction of the system in the form of periodic financial collapse. Unfortunately, predatory operators possess none of the above-mentioned virtues – honesty, integrity and a sense of justice.

Short of selective breeding to remove aggressive traits, capitalistic societies must establish clear-cut, economic rules and regulations to rein in predatory aggression in favor of the most rational, stable economic system for all. Those inclined can still make millions but in an honest, productive way defined by the rules.

In short, the 2007-10(?) financial mess is just the most recent example of a corruption-ridden US Congress doing legislative favors for the predatory financial operators to make lots of money and stick the taxpayer and the country's future with the bill for their financially irresponsible behavior. It is also, however, a once-in-a-century opportunity to reform a corrupt Congress, discard the mindset lunacy of industry (and Congress) of self-regulation and recognize that any expansive attempts in the economy have always resulted in profits for the rich and contractive misery for the rest of us.

Recommended Reading

Anderson, Benjamin M., 1949, *Economics and the Public Welfare,* D. VanNostrand, Princeton, NJ

Chandler, Lester V., 1978, *Benjamin Strong, Central Banker* Arno Press, NJ

Friedman, Milton, 1992, *Money Mischief,* Harcourt, Brace, Jovanovich, NY

Galbraith, John K., 1988, *The Great Crash 1929* Houghton Mifflin, Boston

Greenspan, Alan, 2007, *The Age of Turbulence* Penguin Press, NY

Harris, Seymour E., 1933, *Twenty Years of Federal Reserve Policy,* Harvard University Press, Cambridge, Mass

Lorant, Stephan, 1968, *The Glorious Burden* Harper & Row, NY

Mason, Alpheus T., 1965, *Free Government in the Making,* 3rd ed., Oxford University Press, NY

Ney, Richard, 1970, *The Wall Street Jungle,* Grove Press, NY

Paul, Ron, 2009, *End the Fed,* Grand Central Pub., NY

Samuelson, Robert J., 2008, *The Great Inflation and its Aftermath,* Random House, NY

Shlaes, Amity, 2007, *The Forgotten Man,* Harper Collins, NY

Schroeder, Alice, 2008, *The Snowball [*Warren Buffett*]*Random House, NY

Veblen, Thorstein, 1973, *The Theory of the Leisure Class* (Reprint) Houghton Mifflin, Boston, Mass

Woodward, Bob, 2000, *Maestro [*Alan Greenspan*]*Simon & Schuster, NY

Note: The opinions herein are the author's. Facts and figures have been gleaned and integrated from the above-mentioned books as well as from other media sources.

Made in the USA
Monee, IL
04 November 2026

67377443R00075